Fulfilling THE Promise OF THE Differentiated Classroom

Strategies and Tools for Responsive Teaching

Carol Ann Tomlinson

Association for Supervision and Curriculum Development
Alexandria, Virginia USA

®

Association for Supervision and Curriculum Development
1703 N. Beauregard St. • Alexandria, VA 22311-1714 USA
Telephone: 800-933-2723 or 703-578-9600 • Fax: 703-575-5400
Web site: http://www.ascd.org • E-mail: member@ascd.org

Gene R. Carter, *Executive Director;* Nancy Modrak, *Director of Publishing;* Julie Houtz, *Director of Book Editing & Production;* Tim Sniffin, *Project Manager;* Shelley Young, *Senior Graphic Designer;* Barton Matheson Willse & Worthington, *Typesetter;* Vivian Coss, *Production Specialist.*

ISBN: 0-87120-812-1   ASCD product no.: 103107
ASCD member price: $20.95   nonmember price: $25.95   s11/2003

Library of Congress Cataloging-in-Publication Data
Tomlinson, Carol A.
   Fulfilling the promise of the differentiated classroom : strategies and tools for
responsive teaching / Carol Ann Tomlinson.
      p. cm.
Includes bibliographical references and index.
   ISBN 0-87120-812-1 (alk. paper)
   1. Individualized instruction.   2. Mixed ability grouping in education.   I. Title.

LB1031.T655 2003
371.39'4—dc22

                                                                    2003018530

13 12 11 10 09 08 07 06 05 04 03   12 11 10 9 8 7 6 5 4 3 2 1

For Cindy Strickland and Ellen Hench
Thank you for being my teachers!

I Am A Child

I am a child.
I come to you, a teacher.
I bring a whisper.
Can you hear the poem in it?

I am a child.
I come to you, a teacher.
Will you tell me what to think,
Or show me how?
Will you teach me answers,
Or the symmetry of a question well composed?

I am a child.
I come to you, a teacher.
Will learning be only about doing things right,
Or about doing the right thing?
A thing of joy,
Or of duty?

I am a child.
I come to you, a teacher.
Which will matter most to you,
My soul,
Or my grade?

I am a child.
I come to you, a teacher.
Can you teach me to chart my journey,
Or must you use a standard measure
To place me always
In the shadow of others?

I am a child.
I come to you, a teacher.
Will I go away from you ascending my strengths,
Or hobbled by my weaknesses?

I am a child.
I come to you, a teacher.
I bring you all I am,
All I can become.
Do you understand the trust?

Fulfilling the Promise of the Differentiated Classroom

Acknowledgments

In the Rodgers and Hammerstein musical *The King and I*, Anna sings a simple line that is profoundly true, "If you become a teacher, by your pupils you'll be taught." That, of course, is one of the prime perks of teaching.

I've been reminded of that truth virtually every day of a 30-plus-year career in teaching. It was true when I taught high school students, preschoolers, middle schoolers—and no less so in my more recent years of teaching adults. On my best days as a teacher, I learn more than I teach.

Much of the impetus for this book has come from the excellent work two of my doctoral students have done with me over the last three or four years. I don't mean they've done excellent work *for* me (although they have, of course). I really do mean the work they have done *with* me—or perhaps *within* me. In other words, *they* have been *my* teachers.

Whether because of personality, modeling, setting, or some combination of those elements, it has been a given to me throughout my career that good teaching begins with good relationships between and among teacher and students. Said another way, positive affect has always been for me the foundational ingredient in effective teaching—the "mother sauce" for whatever would be "served up" in the classroom. Likewise, the learning environment has always occupied a sizeable portion of my teacher mind. How do I make this place work for the child who can't sit still? How do I arrange time so I can make meaningful contact with 150 individuals in some reasonable span of time? How do I help students develop the same kind of pride I have in this classroom and its inhabitants?

Positive affect and learning environments became automatics for me somewhere along the line—and pretty early in my career, as I recall. It's not, to say the least, that I had all the answers or always did the right things. I just always understood the need to keep at it. Later, I did what all of us do when we reach a stage of automaticity of performance in any arena: I worked with affect and learning environment without articulating what I did.

Enter two doctoral students at the University of Virginia. Cindy Strickland and Ellen Hench have a passion for the role of affect and learning environments in effective classrooms. For them, it is unthinkable that these two elements might not be articulated as central to any educational endeavor. In their own quiet (and persistent) ways, they continued to say to me, "You can't take it for granted that everyone understands the role of those elements in classrooms."

Cindy and Ellen were reminding me that my work on differentiation was incomplete if it did not squarely and unambiguously address the role of positive affect and learning environment in responsive teaching. About the same time, I was working with a group of teachers in Chapel Hill, North Carolina. One day, we were examining the need to be very specific when crafting product assignments for learners. At lunch, a veteran teacher said to me, "I had one of the most important 'ah-has' of my teaching career today."

"Tell me about it," I said.

"I'm embarrassed to tell you," she responded. "It sounds so silly."

I assured her that an insight that was important to her was not likely to sound silly, and so she took the chance. "What I figured out today," she explained, "is

that it's the teacher's job to make explicit that which we hoped was implicit."

She's right, of course. It's a brilliant insight, and a tough one to practice. Surely the students know what we teachers mean. We've been talking about "it" for so many years. And besides, wouldn't anyone just know to do those things?

It's what Cindy and Ellen were saying to me. "It's your job to make explicit those things about differentiation you assumed were evident to everyone. They are not always evident!" This book, then, finds me laying out the role of learning and environment in differentiation more fully than I have done before. The book also is my opportunity to show how those two elements direct and shape everything else that we value in the classroom. They are, in effect, the catalysts for effective differentiation.

So, along with my enduring gratitude to the folks at ASCD for continued support in developing the concept of differentiation, and colleagues who nurture, challenge and support me, my thanks go to two of my most excellent teachers—Cindy Strickland and Ellen Hench. Their own words will add someday to what I have tried to do here. In the meantime, thanks for the nudge that has made me realize we should never take for granted that something is obvious.

1

What's Behind the Idea of Differentiated Classrooms?

Schools are like airport hubs; student passengers arrive from many different backgrounds for widely divergent destinations. Their particular takeoffs into adulthood will demand different flight plans (Levine, 2002, p. 336).

The idea of differentiating instruction to accommodate the different ways that students learn involves a hefty dose of common sense, as well as sturdy support in the theory and research of education (Tomlinson & Allan, 2000; Tomlinson, et al., in press). It is an approach to teaching that advocates active planning for student differences in classrooms. It suggests, for example:

- If a student learns faster than a prescribed pace or is ready for greater depth or breadth of knowledge than is planned for a learning sequence, those things matter and there should be plans for adapting the pace and scope of learning for that student.
- If a student has great difficulty learning—for whatever reason—there should be provisions made to ensure that the student masters essential knowledge and has an active support system both to fill in gaps in knowledge and to move ahead.
- If a student is just learning to speak English, there should be mechanisms in place to help the student manage critical elements of subject matter as well as practice continually with the new language.
- If a student's culture or gender results in learning preferences that vary from those typically addressed in the classroom, the range of learning modes should be expanded to support effective and efficient learning for each learner.
- If a student has "given up" on school, there should be active and continual planning to help the student reconnect with the power of learning to positively shape his or her life.

In other words, the philosophy of differentiation proposes that what we bring to school as learners matters in how we learn. Therefore, to teach most effectively, teachers must take into account *who* they are teaching as well as *what* they are teaching. The goal of a differentiated classroom is to plan actively and consistently to help each learner move as far and as fast as possible along a learning continuum. The current interest in differentiation is probably a response to several factors in contemporary schools:

- The number of English language learners in classrooms across the country is increasing, even in localities where there were virtually no such students just a few years ago (Center for Immigration Studies, 2001). English language learners face the daunting task of mastering complex subject matter even as they tackle a new language.
- The achievement gap for minority learners—particularly African American, Native American, and Hispanic students—continues in schools across the country (Haycock, 2001). Even accounting for economic status does not eradicate the gap in achievement for these students compared to their Caucasian counterparts (McWhorter, 2001; North Carolina Commission, 2001). The intractability of the gap is probably explained in part by the fact that currently 75 percent of teachers in the United States are Caucasian, while projections are that 70 percent of the student population will be non-Caucasian within the next 25 years (Ginsberg & Wlodkowski, 2000; Garcia, 2002). This mismatch in experience and perspective between many teachers and their students may result in classrooms that are ill suited to the needs of large groups of learners.

- The field of special education has moved steadily toward the goal of inclusive instruction for many students with disabilities; the number of such learners educated in regular classrooms has grown 20 percent over the past decade (U.S. Department of Education, 2000). This approach to the education of students with special education identification is based on the premise that all students—including those with disabilities—are an important part of general education, both benefiting and benefiting from interactions with a wide variety of learners (Shea and Bauer, 1997). At the same time that the field of special education has moved toward inclusion, there are more students with learning problems attending schools (Gersten, et al., 2001; Sternberg & Grigorenko, 2001).
- Our brightest students may be losing academic and motivational ground in classrooms ill-equipped to ensure that they, like other students, are expected to progress at least a year's worth in an academic year (Callahan, et al., 2000).

These factors, of course, only extend the challenge that has always existed for teachers—being many things to many different young learners. The one-size-fits-all teacher may very well discover that the "size" of instruction he or she has selected fits almost no one.

Differentiating Instruction: What and Why

Differentiated instruction is responsive instruction. It occurs as teachers become increasingly proficient in understanding their students as individuals, increasingly comfortable with the meaning and structure of the disciplines they teach, and increasingly expert at teaching flexibly in order to match instruction to student need with the goal of maximizing the potential of each learner in a given area.

More complete explanations of differentiation are available in a variety of sources (e.g., Gartin, et al., 2002; Tomlinson, 1999; Tomlinson, 2001; Tomlinson & Allan, 2000). The goal of this book is to expand on rather than reiterate those explanations. Nonetheless, it is useful to review briefly some common terms related to differentiation and to revisit briefly why particular elements are significant in addressing academic diversity.

Student Traits

There are four student traits that teachers must often address to ensure effective and efficient learning. Those are *readiness, interest, learning profile*, and *affect*. The first three of these student needs have been discussed extensively in the previous publications on this model of differentiation. The fourth, *affect*, will be discussed more extensively throughout this book.

Readiness refers to a student's knowledge, understanding, and skill related to a particular sequence of learning. A student's general cognitive proficiency affects his or her readiness, but readiness is also profoundly influenced by a student's prior learning and life experiences, attitudes about school, and habits of mind. This model of differentiation uses the term *readiness* rather than *ability* because

ability generally seems more fixed, less amenable to intervention, whereas readiness can vary widely over time, topic, and circumstance. Only when a student works at a level of difficulty that is both challenging and attainable for that student does learning take place (Howard, 1994; Jensen, 1998; National Research Council, 1999; Sousa, 2001; Vygotsky, 1962, 1978; Wolfe, 2001). Thus, if readiness levels in a class vary, so must the complexity of work provided for students.

Interest refers to those topics or pursuits that evoke curiosity and passion in a learner. These are facets of learning that invite students to invest their time and energy in the pursuit of knowledge, understanding, and skill. Students bring to school interests in particular areas. School also offers the opportunity for students to realize new interests. Thus, highly effective teachers attend both to developing interests and as yet undiscovered interests in their students. Students whose interests are tapped and deepened in school are more likely to be engaged and to persist in learning (Csikszentmihalyi, 1990; Maslow, 1962; Sousa, 2001; Wolfe, 2001).

Learning profile refers to how students learn best. Preferences for learning are shaped by a constellation of overlapping and interlocking student factors. Those include learning style, intelligence preference, culture, and gender. If classrooms can offer and support different modes of learning, it is likely that more students will learn more effectively and efficiently (Campbell & Campbell, 1999; Sternberg, Torff, & Grigorenko, 1998; Sullivan, 1993).

Affect has to do with how students feel about themselves, their work, and the classroom as a whole. What excites one student about spelling may discourage another, or what makes one student feel successful may discourage another. A teacher in a differentiated classroom attends to student emotions or feelings (affect) as well as to student cognition. In fact, the two are inextricably bound. Positive student affect is far more likely to support student learning than is negative, or even neutral, affect (Given, 2002; Wolfe, 2001). This book will argue that student affect is the gateway to helping each student become more fully engaged and successful in learning.

Classroom Elements

As teachers respond to the four student traits that call for flexible, responsive, or differentiated instruction, there are also four classroom elements they can modify in response to variations among students. Those are *content, process, product*, and *learning environment*. Again, earlier publications on this model of differentiation have explored the first three elements in some detail. The classroom element not discussed as thoroughly is the learning environment, and this book will develop more fully its role in effectively differentiated classrooms.

Content refers to what teachers teach (or, what we want students to learn) and how students gain access to that body of knowledge. In general, it is a goal of differentiation (because it is a goal of school) to enable students to focus and build on the essential information, ideas, and skills of a lesson or unit. That goal is generally feasible to the degree that teachers are clear on what is truly essential about a given learning sequence. In those instances, teachers do not vary so much *what* they are teaching as how students *encounter* the information. To ensure that all students can gain access to the essentials, a teacher might, for example:

- Use visuals or graphic organizers while lecturing—thus engaging both visual and auditory learning modes;
- Ask students to use manipulatives or role playing as a way of understanding a text or oral explanation—thus combining kinesthetic and visual or auditory learning modes;
- Provide taped passages of text, completely taped chapters and books, or use small group instruction to enable students with encoding difficulties to hear rather than read material that would otherwise be inaccessible; and
- Provide some text or supplementary materials in a student's native language, while that student learns to read and speak English, to assist understanding of required English materials.

There are many ways a teacher can ensure that each student has meaningful access to content. There are times, however, when providing varied access to the same content may not be adequate. At those points, the teachers will need to vary the actual content.

For example, a student with serious cognitive challenges and who is in an inclusive classroom may need a separate math curriculum some or all of the time. If the student does not yet have the concept of numbers, it is inadequate simply to use manipulatives to try to teach that student to multiply. The student's current readiness to learn multiplication is so far from the learning goals that it makes no sense to try to teach him all of the same content at the same time and same pace as others in the class.

Similarly, a 1st grader who already reads at a 3rd grade level does not need the same reading skills lessons as many classmates in her 1st grade room. A Spanish-speaking student may be appropriately enrolled in Spanish I, because he does not know the formal grammar of Spanish. It is probably not useful, however, for the student to spend days practicing numbers, days of the week, months of the year, and so on. In such instances, the teacher will be more effective if she varies *what* the student learns rather than simply how the student gains access to knowledge.

Process refers to how a student makes sense of, or comes to understand, the information, ideas, and skills that are at the heart of a lesson. A class activity is an example of process, as is a homework assignment. Effective process ensures that students grapple with, apply, or otherwise make meaning of the information, ideas, and skills essential to a lesson.

Product, in this differentiation model, refers to assessments or demonstrations of what students have come to know, understand, and be able to do as the result of an extended sequence of learning. A product is the student's opportunity to show what she has learned throughout a unit or a semester in history, for example. It is the teacher's evidence of a student's ability to organize and use the knowledge, information, and skill central to a unit or an academic interval, such as a quarter. While an activity (process) will often ask students to produce a tangible outcome, here product does not describe what a student produces at the end of a day or two of learning. Rather, product describes a major assessment. Effective products hold students accountable for using the foundational information, understandings, and skills of the unit (or other extended learning sequence). Products can take such forms as student projects, authentic assessments, tests, solutions to problem-based inquires, exhibitions, portfolios, and so on.

Learning Environment has to do with both the operation and the tone of a classroom. Learning environment is the "weather" that affects virtually everything that transpires in the classroom. Rules for members of the class, furniture arrangement, guidelines for how to get help with work, procedures for passing out and collecting materials, and so on, are part of learning environment. A key ingredient in the learning environment is the "mood" of the classroom. Is the classroom one that balances seriousness about work with celebration of success— or one in which there is a great deal of "loose" time and a sense of obligation and drudgery about work? Is there consistent evidence of respect for everyone in the classroom—or does this seem to be a place where some students seem favored, while some appear out of favor with the teacher or peers or both? Does everyone in the classroom share responsibility for the operation of the class, or is the teacher responsible for making everything in the classroom work? Both the more concrete operation of the classroom and the more abstract classroom tone profoundly affect the potential for responsive teaching.

Linking Student Traits and Classroom Elements

In differentiated classrooms, teachers continually assess student readiness, interest, learning profile, and affect. Teachers then use what they learn to modify content, process, product, and the learning environment to ensure maximum learning for each member of the class. Figure 1.1 provides a few examples of ways in which a teacher might modify classroom elements based on learner needs.

Metaphors to Guide Thinking About Differentiation

Sometimes, metaphors extend our thinking as well as our language. There is a metaphor taken from St. Exupery's book *The Little Prince* that both grounds and extends thinking about differentiation or responsive teaching in the classroom. This metaphor ultimately suggests a second metaphor that will guide thinking about differentiation in this book. The remainder of this chapter will examine both metaphors and how they can begin to guide our thinking about differentiation.

Taming the Fox

The Little Prince, a young boy who is in many ways representative of all of us,

goes on a pilgrimage to make sense of life. In particular, he needs to understand what love means in the scope of his existence. Along the way, he meets and learns from a varied lot of folks—both wise and foolish. Near the end of his journey, he encounters a fox and asks the fox to play with him. The fox responds that he cannot play with the Little Prince because he—the fox—is not tamed. The Little Prince is puzzled and asked what it means to be tamed. The fox responds that it means to establish ties—an act too often neglected, he observes:

> To me, you are still nothing more than a little boy who is just like a hundred thousand other little boys. And I have no need of you. And you, on your part, have no need of me. To you, I am nothing more than a fox like a thousand other foxes. But if you tame me, then we shall need each other. To me, you will be unique in all the world. . . .
>
> My life is very monotonous. . . . And, in consequence, I am a little bored. But if you tame me, it will be as if the sun came to shine on my life. I shall know the sound of a step that will be different from all the others. Other steps send me hurrying back underneath the ground. Yours will call me, like music, out of my burrow. (p. 80, 83)

But the Little Prince is skeptical. He is very busy, he explains. He has so many things to do—so many things to understand. The fox gives a simple reply: "One only understands the things one tames" (p. 83). The Little Prince agrees to tame the fox.

The fox explains that taming takes time, patience, and listening. Words, he notes, are often the source of misunderstanding. In time, the Little Prince tames

FIGURE 1.1

Examples of Modifying Classroom Elements
Based on Learner Need

Student Need	Modification of Classroom Element in Response to Student Need
A spelling pre-assessment indicates that students in a 6th grade class range from 2nd grade level to beyond high school level.	The teacher uses a spelling procedure that involves all students in spelling at the same time, but on varied levels of complexity of words required. (Modification of content based on student readiness.)
Students in a pre-algebra class have varied interests and often have difficulty understanding why they are learning what they are learning in math.	The teacher uses examples from sports, business, medicine, technology, and other fields to illustrate how formulas are used. She also guides students in interviewing people engaged in a range of jobs and hobbies to find out how they use formulas in their work and in sharing those examples with others in the class. (Modification of content and product based on student interest.)
Some students in Advanced Placement History are taking their first advanced course and sometimes feel lost and discouraged by the course's demands.	The teacher establishes study groups to help students prepare for both oral and written tests. Although much of the work of the study groups takes place outside of class, the teacher conducts whole-class and small-group discussions about how the various groups approach studying, how the different approaches seem to work, and how students feel about their progress. He also provides study guides to ensure focus on critical facets of the content. (Modification of learning environment and process based on student readiness and affect.)
Students in 3rd grade are studying biography. Student reading levels vary widely and their interests do as well.	The teacher develops boxes of biographies of people from a range of cultures, both genders, and a variety of jobs and hobbies. In each box are books that span a four- or five-year reading range. Students first select the topic or interest box from which they would like to work and then the teacher helps them pick a book that is a close match for their reading levels. (Modification of content based on student interest and readiness.)
Two students in the class have difficulty with impulsive behavior.	The teacher and students develop goals for behavior and plans for decreasing impulsivity. Both positive and negative consequences of behaviors are described in the goal statements. Students and teacher use a checklist each day to record successes and difficulties as well as the consequence of student choices. (Modification of learning environment based on student affect.)

(continues)

FIGURE 1.1 CONTINUED

Student Need	Modification of Classroom Element in Response to Student Need
In math currently, students need different amounts of time and support to master the concept they are studying.	The teacher does some whole-class teaching every few days. In between, students sometimes work independently at learning centers, sometimes with peers on targeted tasks, and sometimes with the teacher. The teacher adjusts the rotation so students get the amount and kind of work and support they need. (Modification of learning environment and process based on readiness.)
Students often finish their work at different times.	The teacher establishes several areas of the room where students may work when they have time. There are a variety of tasks in each area based on both what students need to work on and what they most enjoy working on. Sometimes students select where to work. Sometimes the teacher asks students to work in a particular area and on a particular task. (Modification of learning environment and process based on student readiness and interest.)
Students in the science class seem to learn best through different means.	The teacher develops a procedure he calls "Learning x3." Periodically during a unit, he asks students to explain what's essential in what they are learning. They may write their explanation, provide it verbally, or do a demonstration as an explanation. There are criteria for quality that span all three approaches. He groups the students in threes so that each triad contains all three approaches to the explanation. As students share, he monitors the groups and selects one student to represent each approach before the whole class. (Modification of process based on learning profile.)
Five students in class have great difficulty with writing—some because of learning problems and some because they are learning English.	The teacher posts lists of key words for each unit on the wall. She also supports students in first webbing their ideas for writing, then tape recording the ideas, and then writing the ideas. Students may get help in writing or editing from peers, specialists when they are scheduled into the classroom, and the teacher at specified times. (Modification of process and learning environment based on student readiness.)
Students in Art I vary greatly in skill and experience with art as they enter the class.	The teacher uses rubrics that specify key skills on which students need to work as well as describing what ascending proficiency looks like for each skill. Each student works with the teacher to set proficiency goals for products based on the student's current work. Grading is based on both individual growth and grade-level benchmarks. (Modification of product based on student readiness.)

the fox, who shares with his new friend two important truths:

1. "What is essential is invisible to the eye," (p. 87) and
2. "You become responsible forever for what you have tamed." (p. 88)

In the end, the fox and Little Prince must part ways, of course. There is great sadness in the parting, but there is happiness born of fulfillment as well. The two will be joined forever by the small memories they made together—the times they shared.

The Little Prince and Differentiation

Children spend the majority of their waking hours in schools and classrooms. They are dependent on the adults who shape the experience in those schools and classrooms for the quality of each day spent there.

When they enter the classroom, the teacher says to them, "Come play with me"; "Come do the work I have for you here"; "Make my agenda your agenda."

It is likely that each child says to us in his or her own way, "I can't do that until you have tamed me. I can't give myself to this place, to this work, to you until I believe in you. I can't believe in you until I know you believe in me." In 30 different ways, students in a class of 30 say to the teacher, like the fox, "Tame me, please." They want to feel a personal connection to those who share the classroom with them. They want to be affirmed there.

Like the Little Prince, teachers are skeptical. We have so many things to do,

so many things to understand, too many mandates, too many students, too little time in days that evaporate time. But if we take the risk to "tame" each child who comes our way, the uniqueness of every individual emerges. It happens because we show up each day with patience, with the intent to listen. We make time to "see the invisible."

In that process, we begin to understand what makes a creative child unique, what a child with cognitive limitations needs from the classroom to grow, how the culture of a child is shaped by experiences both like and unlike our own, what the very bright child needs to feed both intellect and a sense of belonging, how a student's particular interest represents that child's dreams, and so on. We begin to understand what is essential about each learner.

If we risk taming the fox, days in school are no longer monotonous. Each day is a revelation. School not only enables the child to become what he might be, but it involves the child in observing and contributing to the metamorphosis.

There is risk, of course. Perhaps our efforts will be rejected. Perhaps we will fail at creating ties with some students. Our colleagues may even disparage our efforts as an endeavor costly in time and emotion. In any case, it is wearying always to be taming. And like the fox and Little Prince, the student and teacher must part ways in the end. There is a summer, and we must begin the taming all over again, even as we mourn those who left us behind. If we have connected with the students who left, we *do* mourn their parting, or at least feel a sense of incompleteness at not being able to continue to shepherd them, not being able to continue to shape and to follow their journeys. The fox was correct: We do feel responsible forever for those we tame.

There is an interesting twist in the metaphor about taming the fox that seems, at first, to challenge the appropriateness of the metaphor for thinking about differentiation. The Little Prince is the one who tames the fox—the one who responds to the fox's plea to be tamed. That would make the Little Prince analogous to the teacher in a classroom. Yet it is the fox who seems to do much of the teaching in the story. Shouldn't the Little Prince be the wise one, the teacher whose words become legend?

In this story, it is interesting that both parties are teachers and both are learners. Their roles mingle and reverse. They are partners in what transpires. Creating ties presents risks to both. Both listen. Both exemplify patience. Both anticipate the days they spend together. Both are hurt at the parting. Both are enriched by what they share. Both are givers and receivers.

The Little Prince succeeds in his taming of the fox. In other words, he fulfills the teacher's role effectively. A closer look at the metaphor affirms that it is the Little Prince who is officially the teacher. A closer look reminds us, however, that teachers who are willing to establish ties with students discover new depths of truth each day that they take the risk of practicing their profession. There are, of course, things teachers are supposed to know—ideas, skills, understandings they are charged with transmitting to the young.

Such teachers are willing to be vulnerable learners. The puzzle pieces of knowledge and ideas they "own" make sense more fully—to teacher as well as student—when combined with the mysteries of each of the lives in the classroom.

The concept of differentiating instruction for varied learners has its roots in the belief that we teach best when we accept the need to tame the fox. That is, we teach responsively when we understand the need to teach the human beings before us as well as to teach the content with which we are charged. In a time when teachers feel almost unbearable pressure to standardize what we do, it is important to begin with the conviction that we are no longer teaching if what we teach is more important than who we teach or how we teach.

A Clockwork of Three Cogs

A second metaphor is also helpful in understanding the genesis and intent of differentiation. It is a "clockwork" of three cogs—interrelated and interdependent—that depicts key elements in the classroom (see Figure 1.2).

Working with the assumption that the request to tame the fox is central to what happens in a classroom, the first of the three cogs represents the needs of the student in the classroom. The second cog represents the role of the teacher in the classroom. The third represents the role of curriculum and instruction in the classroom.

In the first cog, the student seeks

- affirmation,
- contribution,

- power,
- purpose, and
- challenge.

This list may be conceived in somewhat different ways. For instance, each teacher might revise the list a bit based on personal philosophy and experience. Nonetheless, the list gives us a good starting point for exploring the human needs students bring to the classrooms in which they invest 13 years. The premise

of differentiation is that we cannot teach nearly so well when we overlook or under-attend to these student needs. Indeed, they are the gateway to learning.

In the second cog, a teacher who intends to connect with students inevitably and willfully responds to their needs through

- invitation,
- opportunity,
- investment,

FIGURE 1.2
The Cogs of Differentiation

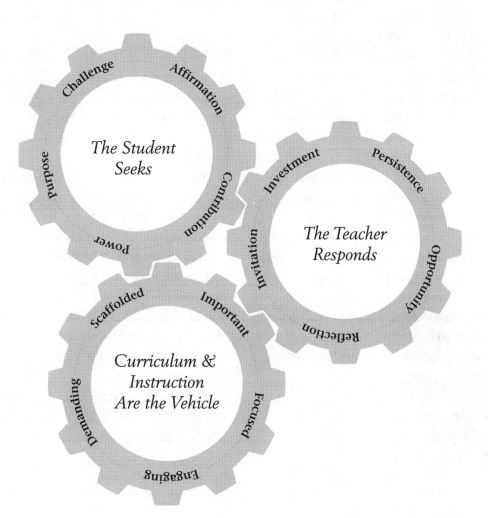

- persistence, and
- reflection.

Once again, this list might be modified somewhat, depending on the perspective of a given educator. Nonetheless, these are appropriate teacher responses to what a student seeks. Understanding these elements can provide us with a compass for decision making as a teacher plans to adapt instruction to student needs.

School, however, does not exist to be a cocoon or to substitute for a psychologist's office—although both elements are arguably represented in effective classroom environments. A distinctive responsibility of schools is to help young people develop the knowledge, skills, and understandings to contribute to society. Thus, curriculum and instruction are central in the mission of schools. The concept of differentiation affirms the centrality of curriculum and instruction in classrooms. Differentiation calls on teachers to understand that curriculum and instruction also are the teacher's medium for attending to what the learner seeks. In other words, the most effective teaching does not seek transmission of knowledge isolated from human need, but rather attempts to help young learners discover the power of knowledge to reveal, amplify, and develop the best that is in them. To that end, curriculum in a differentiated classroom—the third cog—will be

- important,
- focused,
- engaging,
- demanding, and
- scaffolded.

As in the case of the elements that define students needs and teacher response to them, the elements that describe curriculum and instruction could be modified somewhat based on the vantage point of the teacher. Nonetheless, these five elements—as is the case with the student and teacher elements—are rooted in our current understanding of the psychology of teaching and learning, our escalating knowledge of the brain, and our long experience in observing and learning from daily interactions in countless classrooms.

An effectively differentiated classroom is not simply one that seeks to balance the elements of student need, teacher response, and the role of curriculum and instruction. Rather, it is a classroom in which it is clear that unless the three elements remain carefully calibrated to work in concert, each element will inevitably be reduced to less than it ought to be.

The remainder of this book will draw on the two metaphors of taming the fox and the connected cogs as a means of helping educators to understand more fully what it means to teach responsively—to teach in an effectively differentiated way. To do that, the book will explore both the theory and practice that undergird differentiation. To deal with both seems critical to informed classroom practice. In an e-mail message, California educator Jill Carroll captures the need for practice supported by theory, and theory translated into practice:

> A group of differentiated activities, without teachers understanding and embracing the rationale and reason-

ing behind them, comprise little more than a cookbook. Once the activities have all been used, teachers have no way to generate others effectively. I also find that without understanding the theoretical underpinnings (of differentiation), teachers are likely to modify an activity in a way that defeats its purpose. On the other hand, if only theory and generic strategies are offered without concrete examples, teachers lack the time for reflection, experimentation, and creation of materials to bridge the gap. If teachers have both theory and examples, they can modify the activities to fit their teaching styles and students' needs, and can do so across subject areas (personal communication, April 2002).

To that end, the chapters that follow explore both the *why* of differentiated teaching (its theory) and the *how* (its practice). Their aim is to help interested educators extend the responsiveness of their teaching in reasoned ways.

2

Student Needs as the Impetus for Differentiation

"Claude," he called, "I'm going to learn French so I can read your book. And I'm going to read at school, study. I'm going to learn everything for this orchard." No more looking out the window at school, he thought. No more dreaming. His orchard (Giff, 2001, p. 157).

Every year as a new school year begins, teachers around the country—and the world—issue the same invitation to a new group of essentially indistinguishable students: "Come play with me. Come do the work I have planned for you. Come learn what I have designated as important."

No doubt there are always a few students who run right into the room saying, "Sure! Whatever you say, I'm with you." Most children, however, are more reluctant to give themselves unequivocally to the demands of school.

Even on the surface, that is not hard to understand. For our youngest students, school means being one of many rather than only one, or one of a precious few. They might say, "School means losing so many of the choices I was just getting the hang of at home. School means my bedroom and my toys and my favorite snacks are far away. School means I have to get up and get dressed even when I feel very tired—and once there, it means I have to do work that doesn't much resemble the play that was so satisfying at home. Often it means that when I do get back home, I have to take school with me and do more work that someone else thinks is important and lose more time with my family and for play."

Older students are more accustomed to the separation from the familiar that school brings. Even so, they might say, "It's a plus that school puts me in proximity to my friends. Yet, the schedule is still someone else's. The work is something imposed on me. The content seems more remote from my life as it gets more complex, and my schoolwork takes up so much time and energy. In the end, I somehow don't see my friends much of the day. A bell rings, and I move on. I go to class and sit. Another bell rings, and I move on again. And now, I notice a pattern emerging about school and my life. If people judge me as successful in school, I must maintain that success at all costs. If

14

people judge me as unsuccessful, won't I *always* be considered a failure?"

"Come play with me," says the teacher. "Come do what I ask you to do."

"I can't," says the student, "at least not until you connect with me. Oh, I'll go through the motions, of course. But *give* myself to this adult thing called school? Not unless you connect with me."

What the Student Needs

Many years ago, Abraham Maslow (1962) helped us understand that until a human has basic human needs attended to, until that human feels safe, until that human feels a sense of belonging, energies cannot go to learning. Much more recently, researchers who study the brain and authors who interpret their work for educators have told us that emotions trump learning. If a child feels unsafe, threatened, or insecure, the brain blocks off the pathways to learning and attends to the more basic human needs instead (Given, 2002; Sousa, 2001; Wolfe, 2001). If a teacher connects learning to a child's emotions, she is more likely to learn than if what is being taught remains remote from her emotions (Wolfe, 2001). It is as

though a voice deep inside the learner says, "First, protect yourself. Take care of yourself." In this way, learners are egocentric and self-centered (see Figure 2.1). Far from being undesirable, this focus on the self is a matter of preserving the core of one's being.

Learners young and old, then, come into the classroom with uncertainty. "How is it going to be for me in here?" they ask. "If what we do here meets my needs to be safe, to become stronger, I'm with you. If not, I can be simultaneously present in the room and absent from what you are asking of me."

There are at least five needs learners seek to meet. Students do not enter classrooms saying, "Please teach me to multiply fractions. That seems so significant to me!" They do not arrive at the door saying, "If only you'd teach me about the American Revolution, I would feel whole." Rather, students come to the schoolhouse saying, "Will I be affirmed as a person here? Is there a real contribution for me to make in this place? Will what goes on here seem purposeful to me? Will it make me realize I have power within me? Will I feel a satisfaction that comes from a challenge conquered?"

FIGURE 2.1

Source: PEANUTS © UFS Reprinted by permission.

FIGURE 2.2
The Student Seeks

What Do the Elements Mean?

Affirmation

- I am accepted and acceptable here.
- I am safe here as I am.
- People listen to me here.
- People know how I'm doing, and it matters.
- My interests and perspectives are acknowledged and acted on.
- People believe in me here.

Contribution

- I make a difference in this place and in the work in this place.
- I bring to this place abilities and perspectives that are unique.
- I help others and the class as a whole succeed.
- I am connected to others through mutual work on common goals.

Power

- What I learn is useful to me now.
- I make choices that contribute to my success.
- I understand how this place operates and what is expected of me.
- I know what quality looks like here and how to achieve it.
- There is dependable support here for my journey.

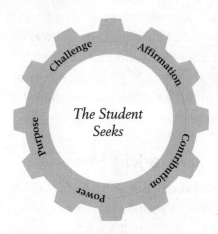

Purpose

- I understand what we do here.
- I see significance in what we do here.
- What we learn reflects me and my world.
- The work we do makes a difference in the world.
- The work absorbs me.

Challenge

- The work here complements my ability.
- The work stretches me.
- I work hard.
- I am accountable for my own growth and contribution to the growth of others.
- I often accomplish things here I didn't believe were possible.

These are questions posed more by emotion—feelings or affect—than by reason or cognition. In other words, the student examines the invitation of the teacher to "come play my game," and says, "Not unless it works for me. Not unless you connect with me."

So what, exactly, does a student need in order to invest repeatedly, consistently, and deeply in school? We'll examine five key needs of learners (see Figure 2.2). Feel free to add others to the list as your knowledge and experience suggest them to you, or to modify the descriptions of the five key needs based on your perspectives.

Affirmation

Perhaps the most basic of student needs is for affirmation. "Am I going to be okay here?" To meet that goal, the student needs to know

- I am accepted and acceptable here;
- I am safe here as I am;
- People listen to me here;
- People know how I'm doing, and it matters to them that I do well;
- People acknowledge my interests, strengths, and perspectives here and draw on them; and
- People believe in me here.

These are basically self-esteem issues. The student is asking, "Do I feel worthy here?" If the answer is too often in the negative, learning necessarily takes a back seat to self-protection.

Contribution

Important as self-esteem is, the developing person must move from its protective cocoon toward a sense of self-efficacy. Each student also needs to know that he can accomplish significant things. Self-efficacy deepens the roots of self-esteem: "Not only do people *tell* me I am worthwhile, I can actually *see* that I am."

Thus, learners come to the classroom needing to make a difference—needing to make a contribution. But learners can also feel that the teacher and class can get along without their contribution. The young person says to the teacher, "Can you do without me here? If so, go right ahead." If he is not needed, he's not in the game.

In regard to the need to contribute, the learner needs to know

- I make a difference in this place and in the work in this place;

- I bring to this place abilities and strengths that are unique;
- Because of these abilities and strengths, I help others in the class and the class as a whole succeed; and
- I am connected to others through mutual work on common goals.

In essence, each learner needs to come to see that he or she is a nonnegotiable part of a classroom system with interdependent parts. The system needs that part—that student—to function effectively and vigorously.

Power

Much of growing up has to do with increasing the dominion one has over one's world. A baby gains a degree of control over her universe when she learns that she can put herself back to sleep after awakening in the night. "It's nice if Mom comes when I cry, but it's not necessary. I can do this for myself," the baby learns. A toddler achieves an empowering milestone when he makes it across the kitchen floor on his own steam. "This room is more mine now than it was before," he understands. And so children want to learn to cross the street so they can go to a neighbor's house. Learning to ride a bicycle broadens the geography of one's world. Talking on the phone, learning to surf the Internet, and driving a car give one vastly more dominion over one's world.

Learners seek power in the classroom as well. "Can you show me how this place and its work give me dominion in my life?" the young person asks. "After all, that's a big part of growing up—of becoming who I need to be." In regard to power in the classroom, the learner needs assurance that

- What I learn is useful to me now;
- I consistently learn to make choices that contribute to my success;
- I understand how this place operates and what is expected of me here;
- I know what quality looks like here and how to achieve it; and
- There is dependable support for my journey here.

When the content and learning environment of a classroom make learners feel powerful, they will likely come back for more power—it is satisfying to find themselves becoming more powerful. If what goes on in the classroom appears to diminish learners' power, they will seek power elsewhere.

Purpose

Young learners seek a sense of purpose in what they do. Purpose, like power and contribution, is a factor in developing a sense of self-efficacy.

"How come we have to do this?" is perhaps the most frequent refrain in any classroom and perhaps the question that most tests teachers. The question does not originate from a student's need to challenge adult authority so much as from a drive to seek meaning. The question could be posed in many ways. "Can you show me how this work helps me become who I want to be?" "Can you show me how this subject contributes to the betterment of people's lives." "Can you help me understand how this rule

makes us more viable as a group?" All those versions of the "How come we've got to do this" question are asked in search of purpose.

As they seek purpose, young learners need to realize

- I understand what we do here;
- What we do here reflects me and my world;
- What we do here helps me make meaning of the subject, my world, and the wider world;
- What we do here makes a difference in the world; and
- The work here absorbs me.

I once had a professor who often would scan a student essay, reflect a moment, scan it again, reflect a bit more, and ultimately look up to ask the bemused student, "Can you help me understand why I should care about this?" It was, of course, a damning question, because it inevitably indicated the student had failed to communicate why it was worth a reader's while to invest time in the piece.

The student's quest for purpose sends him down a similar path. He listens and reflects, does worksheets and reflects, does homework and reflects. At some point he looks up at those of us who teach him. "Can you help me understand why I should care about this?" he says.

Challenge

There is something transforming about taking a risk to attain a goal that seems out of reach and discovering that we can extend our reach to grasp what seemed elusive. When life works as it should, we dream dreams, make plans, aspire to be more tomorrow than we were yesterday. We are invigorated by challenge, strengthened by working toward it, and ennobled by attaining it.

Rightly conceived, learning is a sequence of challenges. Students encounter something—a skill, an idea, a problem, a task—for which they are not quite ready. In the face of that challenge, students feel uncertainty, doubt, and perhaps fear. If students do not take the risk, they may feel comfortable but do not grow. If students take repeated risks and repeatedly find success to be elusive, they do not learn what was intended but *do* conclude that learning is not for them. Challenge is highly personal. It is rare when a single classroom task will invite each learner equally to risk uncertainty, persist in the face of doubt, and attain the goal that seemed for a while out of reach.

In regard to challenge in the classroom, a student needs to know

- The work here complements my abilities;
- The work stretches me;
- I work hard here most of the time;
- I am accountable for my own growth and for contributing to the growth of others; and
- I often accomplish things here I didn't believe were possible.

Youth is a time for dreaming. Young people look first at parents, then at a wider circle of family and friends, and ultimately at the world beyond the neighborhood and dream of what might be for

them as their circle of independence expands. Challenge in the classroom gives roots and wings to young dreams. It prepares learners with the substance, habits, and confidence necessary to move toward their dreams.

Differentiation and Student Needs

Those of us who persist in the profession of teaching want students in our classrooms to experience affirmation, contribution, power, purpose, and challenge. It's difficult to imagine a teacher saying, "Look, I just don't care if a student of mine feels affirmed or rejected in my classroom. It simply makes no difference to me if a learner feels challenged." Nonetheless, for many students of all sorts, school falls far short of meeting those five basic needs. It is far more difficult than it would seem to craft classrooms that are generally affirming, empowering, challenging, and so on to the diverse learners in those rooms.

In fact, because students do differ so greatly, the premise of differentiation is that while students have the same *basic* needs, those needs will *manifest themselves* in different ways, depending on the student's gender, culture, general life experiences, talents, interests, learning preferences, affective development, cognitive development, and support systems. Thus, the philosophy of differentiation suggests the same classroom experience often affects different learners in different ways.

Effective differentiation begins with awareness and understanding of basic student needs. It progresses as teachers become more and more adept at understanding how those basic needs are manifested in the classroom and how each facet of classroom experiences meets a learner's need—or misses the mark for that learner.

Same Needs, Different Spins

While all students in a classroom are likely to have the same basic need for affirmation, contribution, power, purpose and challenge, those needs will often—although not always—take on a different "spin" for each student, reflecting her collective life experiences. To understand how classroom experiences filter through a particular student's needs, we'll take a closer look at two students.

DuShawn is an African American male. Bianca is a Hispanic female. They do not represent all African American or Hispanic learners. Rather, their particular ways of looking at the world have been shaped before they came to school by their particular families and their particular cultural circles. While these two students differ from each other in many ways, they are alike in that both entered school with a collective or group orientation. When they arrived at school, they found, by contrast, an emphasis on the individual. Figure 2.3 provides some contrasts between the way DuShawn and Bianca had come to expect the world to operate prior to beginning school and ways they often find school operating.

DuShawn and Bianca, like all other students in their class, need to feel affirmed. In their class, however, they are scolded for using another student's book or pencil without asking. They naturally share their ideas about work with peers, but find they have broken a rule about working alone or silently when they do so. Both students are uncomfortable when they are praised in public for their work. It seems to separate them from their peers.

DuShawn and Bianca are not off base. Neither is their teacher. They simply come to school with some subtle, but powerfully different, presuppositions about how things should be done. Thus, routine learning experiences that may be highly affirming for students whose way of looking at the world matches the teacher's may make DuShawn and Bianca feel awkward, unaccepted, and unacceptable. Over time they may begin to reject the environment and people who make them feel out of step, even though they may not be able to articulate why they feel that way. The teacher simply wants her students to learn to work effectively in a crowded classroom. She has no idea that a key need for DuShawn and Bianca is going unmet.

Other Undetected Student Needs

As teachers, we quickly learn to distinguish days when plans go seriously amok from others when the classroom seems to function smoothly and efficiently. We are likely to make those distinctions by taking snapshots of the class as a whole. "The students" are working with concentration—or they are not. "The students" seem to understand the idea you are teaching—or they do not. At any moment, there are 30 students in the classroom, give or take a few. There are

---
FIGURE 2.3
Contrasts Between DuShawn and Bianca's Cultural and School Perspectives
---

In DuShawn's and Bianca's Cultural Circles	In School
• Emphasis is on the child as a part of the group	• Emphasis is on the child as an individual
• Helpfulness is valued	• Independence is valued
• Correction is used liberally for normative behavior	• Praise is used liberally for self-esteem
• Emphasis is on social skills	• Emphasis is on cognitive skills
• Children listen to authority figures	• Children negotiate with authority figures
• The teacher's role is to educate	• The parent's role includes educating
• Sharing property is paramount	• Personal property is important
• Questioning by adults indicates the adult's need for information	• Questioning by adults is rehearsal for school
• Collaboration and group success are supreme	• Independence and individual success are supreme
• Strengths in practical and creative pursuits are emphasized	• Emphasis on analytical pursuits

Source: Data from Delpit (1995); Heath (1983); Singleton (2001); Sternberg (1999; in press); and Trumbull, Rothstein-Fisch, Greenfield, & Quiroz (2001).

incalculable demands on the attention of the teacher. Snapshot taking will have to do. No time for individual portraits here! Thus we draw group conclusions. If the *class* seems "engaged," that must mean *everyone* is engaged. If the *class* seems "restless," that must mean *everyone* is restless.

In that manner, we also draw conclusions about basic student needs: "I want to affirm my students"; "I want everyone to be a contributor"; "It matters that my

students are challenged"; "I make plans for those things"; "The class seems to be going well. My plans must be working."

Of course, chances are your plans *are* working for many students. Sometimes they are working well for everyone. As with most worthwhile endeavors, the devil is in the fine points. Would we see that DuShawn is feeling uncomfortable in the classroom? Would we understand why? Would we see and understand the silence of a child weighted with fears dragged from home to school? Would we understand the growing disenchantment of a highly creative child with the regimentation of school? To deal with the details is to connect with students. It is to understand that DuShawn is different in some critical ways from every other student in the classroom—even as he is like every other student in some ways. It is to understand that, at some points, virtually every learner is a DuShawn, needing to be seen, understood, and responded to as an individual.

Figure 2.4 examines some brief scenarios that again highlight ways in which individual students may experience the classroom differently than peers and therefore have key needs go unmet—although our snapshots tell us the class is going well.

Looking Back . . . and Ahead

Teaching asks us to do the impossible. It asks us to establish ties with each child—not to establish ties with all the children as though they were one student. They are not.

In the early stages of our teaching, most of us do well to "manage" the students and "cover" the curriculum. There is no time, no energy, no skill for really even seeing, let alone connecting with individual students. If we elect to continue to develop professional expertise, however, we can get better and better first at seeing and then at connecting with children individually. We learn to

listen better, to look beyond the obvious, and to accept the responsibility for each child and the inevitable risk of failure so that we can move ahead toward greater degrees of success toward becoming more effective teachers.

The truth is, we will never really do all each child needs us to do. A simultaneous truth is that the first truth is no reason to stop trying.

In *Educating Esmé*, a powerful diary of a feisty and wise first-year teacher, Esmé Raji Codell (1999) reflects on her proclivity for trying to do the impossible in her classroom:

> Even if I come across as naïve and zealous, even if I get on everyone's nerves, I have to . . . [try]. Even if I fail, I have to try and try and try. It may be exhausting, but that is beside the point. The goal is not necessarily to succeed but to keep trying, to be the kind of person who has ideas and sees them through. We'll see. I aim too high probably. But if I don't aim, how will I hit anywhere near the target (p. 8).

Reflecting on the immensity of the needs of the immense number of students with whom we have worked and will work becomes an easy invitation to teacher guilt. The point is not to entertain guilt. The point is to relentlessly seize the remarkable opportunity of a teacher to shape lives—to do the best we can to ensure that we are better at reaching children today than yesterday, better at it this year than last.

Connecting with *each* child is at the heart of differentiated teaching, because this approach to teaching does not accept learners as interchangeable parts.

FIGURE 2.4

Classroom Scenarios and Students' Needs

Scenario	Student's Experience
Lee is a student with mild retardation. He likes the other students in his class. His teacher is attentive to him and makes sure he is included in student work groups on a routine basis so that he feels a sense of belonging. She has also worked hard to ensure that students are accepting of one another in their groups.	Lee's reaction to group work is different from what his teacher intends. Lee can almost never contribute anything to the group. Everyone else's reading and writing skills surpass his. He generally works slower than his peers. Lee dreads group-work days. He sits on the edge of the group and feels alone. He never has a sense that he makes a positive difference in the group's work
Beth is a very advanced learner. In several subjects she is at least three or four years ahead of grade expectations in knowledge and skill. Her teacher is generous with praise and lets Beth and her parents know how proud she is of the quality of Beth's work. Her teacher wants to be sure to affirm Beth's ability and to give her a sense of the power she has as a learner.	Beth has a sense that she is not important in the classroom. If she were, the teacher would know she is only repeating things she has long since learned rather than challenging herself. The work in the classroom does not seem purposeful to her and does not absorb her. And she somehow feels dishonest because the teacher tells her she is doing excellent work when she knows she makes high grades with no effort. Beth routinely leaves school with needs for affirmation, purpose, and challenge unmet.
Michelle's teacher explains to his students that the work they are doing in class is important for the standardized tests in the spring, additional courses they will need to take to prepare for college, and college admission exams. He tells them stories about students who have come back to tell him that his class contributed to their acceptance in a good college and success once they got to college.	No one in Michelle's family has ever been to college. While she would like to go, it doesn't seem like a viable option. She has no idea how to apply. If she did get in, there would be no money for tuition. Yet her teacher seems to expect everyone in the class to go to college. Does that mean she will let him down? She likes him and doesn't want to do that. Meanwhile, she wonders if anyone ever really uses their studies for anything at all. It all seems so remote from her world. The class makes her feel powerless.

(continues)

—————————— FIGURE 2.4 CONTINUED ——————————

Scenario	Student's Experience
Lydia has a learning disability. Her teacher makes allowances for her by dictating tests. The learning disabilities specialist works with her several times a week on her writing. Her mom works with her at home on homework, so her work is proofread. Everyone is working hard with Lydia to help her compensate for her learning problems.	Lydia works hard, but the work seems so rote. It's the same thing year after year. Her mind thinks about important things, but no one ever asks her to write or think about important things. It all seems like trivia to her. The other students, by contrast, seem to spend more time on ideas and less on spelling and commas and handwriting. Maybe that means she is not really capable of doing important things. Lydia lacks a sense of purpose and cognitive challenge in her work. It makes her think her disability defines her rather than her abilities.
Randall's teacher likes to involve her students in making decisions about the classroom. Whenever she can, she lets the students decide the order in which they will do particular tasks, criteria by which their work should be assessed, due dates for projects, and so on. She also writes to parents and asks them to become involved in their children's writing and projects and to send feedback on their progress.	In Randall's culture, the teacher is seen as the authority figure and should act accordingly. He is confused and ill at ease when the teacher appears to ask students how to run the classroom. Does that mean she doesn't know how? His mother is confused about requests for her to teach her son. She doesn't want to usurp the teacher's role. That would be impolite. Randall senses that his mother doesn't respond the way other mothers do. He's uncomfortable about that and his mother is uncomfortable at parent conferences.

Jane Tompkins (1996) is right. Teaching *is* fundamentally about building lives. Differentiating instruction focuses on the uniqueness of each child's life as well as its commonalities with all other lives. To build lives in a differentiated classroom means building them both collectively and individually.

The chapter that follows examines what a teacher in a differentiated classroom does in a best effort to respond to what a learner seeks. It is the teacher's response that allows us to move beyond the veil of guilt inevitably surrounding a sensitive teacher to concrete action on behalf of the learner.

3

Teacher Response to Student Needs: A Starting Point for Differentiation

The good teacher communicates a deep regard for students' lives, a regard infused with unblinking attention, respect, even awe. An engaged teacher begins with the belief that each student is unique, each the one and only who will ever trod the earth, each worthy of a certain reverence. Regard extends, importantly, to an insistence that students have access to the tools with which to negotiate and transform the world. Love for students just as they are—without any drive or advance toward a future—is false love, enervating and disabling (Ayres, Klonsky, & Lyon, 2000, pp. 2–3).

It is no small thing to ask teachers to be fox tamers—to establish ties with all of their students. Where are they to find the time to form ties with even one student in the press to cover the curriculum, complete paperwork, attend meetings, set up for the next day—and have a life?

The excuses for not connecting personally with students are legion—and not without legitimacy. There *are* too many students. The time *is* too short. There *is* only one level of textbook in the class, only one set of standards for all. The room *is* too small. Materials *are* lacking. Kids *don't* come to us knowing how to be independent learners. We were *not* trained or hired to be social workers or psychologists. We *don't* know how to think about cultures different from our own. We *are* already consumed by the job.

Nonetheless, sometimes we shove past those reservations and make ties with our students. Some of us consistently ignore these reservations and really get to know our students, becoming the kind of teachers who shape their students' lives to reflect a greater hope, confidence, and promise than these young people brought to the classroom as the year began.

What propels some of us to form bonds with kids as a way of life? Perhaps these fox-taming teachers continue to nurture and sustain a greater sense of the full possibilities of school in the lives of young people.

Barbara Kingsolver (1997) reminds us that the very least we ought to expect of ourselves is that we figure out what we hope for in this life. The most we can do, she continues, is to make sure we live inside our hopes,

25

rather than admiring them from a distance. Perhaps those teachers who are successful in forming bonds with students remember the dreams of the novice teacher clearly enough that they inhabit those dreams daily. The way we "do school" often makes it easy to forget why teaching once seemed the best job in the world and makes it easy to lose sight of what we once hoped for.

What *Was* Our Vision for the Classroom?

People enter the teaching profession for various reasons, of course. For many who elect to teach, however, there is an early sense of enormous possibilities arising from the intersection of young energy, adult mentorship of the energy, and the limitless possibilities of learning. In some sort of naïve way, we know as beginning teachers that the classroom is a microcosm of the world; to fashion a dynamic and positive classroom is to contribute in real ways to a more dynamic and positive world. We feel we have the capacity as teachers to both express and extend a vision of the way the world should be (Apple & Beane, 1995).

Although our language for the vision is fuzzy (and our sense of how to accomplish the vision is virtually nonexistent), we sense as novices that we are destined to be much more than dispensers of information, sergeants of behavior, and captains of the test prep. Had we more sophistication, we would agree that classrooms are places designed to forge democracy, dignity, and diversity (Beane, 1990). We would affirm that schools exist to prepare young people to con-

tribute to their world as informed thinkers, thoughtful citizens, and decent human beings—that we are entering a moral contract between ourselves, our students, and our society to contribute in every way possible to those outcomes (Sizer & Sizer, 1999).

When she was told that her faculty was remarkable, Deborah Meier (1995), a remarkable principal and educational visionary, agreed. She explains, however, that her school's staff is not remarkable because they are more gifted than other teachers or because they have taught longer or because they went to more exclusive colleges. They are remarkable, says Meier, because they live what they believe.

Such teachers are surely aware of the constraints and imperfections of schools. Somehow, they see the possibilities more clearly than the impossibilities. They look beyond those things they *cannot* change toward the young people, learning environments, curricula, and instruction they *can* change.

These teachers ultimately say to their students, "I want to be a leader in creating a place where each of you becomes more keenly aware of the possibilities in yourself, the people around you, and the power of knowledge. In this place, I want us to find together a good way to live."

Such teachers are not perfect people. They lose sight of the vision from time to time. When they do, however, they understand that they have lost their compass, and they hunt for "North" until they find their way again. They have no road map for the journey. It is their expectation, nonetheless, that they will learn more than they teach and that each discovery will reveal another step along the way.

Thus, if the student says, "I need affirmation, contribution, power, purpose, and challenge," such a teacher replies, "I will respond to those needs. Otherwise, how would I assume I could truly teach you? Otherwise, how would I assume we could build together a place in which we can all become what we are meant to be?"

Teacher Responses to Student Needs

There are at least five ways in which a teacher can respond to the student's needs for affirmation, contribution, power, purpose, and challenge. They are not ancillary to teaching but are at the core of effective teaching. They are not separate from the learner's needs but are outcroppings of those needs. And as we will see later, they are not apart from curriculum and instruction, but they breathe life into it.

Once again, we'll examine five key teacher responses to student needs (see Figure 3.1). Feel free to add others to the list or to modify it as your knowledge, experience, and perspectives suggest.

The Response of Invitation

If the first request of the child is for affirmation, the first response of the teacher is, "This will be a good place for you." The invitation to learn is of prime importance. It must be issued as the learner first enters the learning place—and reissued continually. Although the learner yearns for connection, it is also a risky endeavor: "What if the teacher looks past me rather than into me?

What if the teacher rejects my culture, is put off by my rough edges? What if my best is deemed inadequate?" Consciously or unconsciously, the young person continues to measure the benefits against the risks. The teacher who intends to make ties with the student is permanently attuned to factors that enhance the invitation and minimize the risk for each learner and for the class as a whole.

To issue the invitation, the teacher's demeanor, words, and actions need to communicate the following:

- I respect who you are as well as who you can become.
- I want to know you.
- You are unique and valuable.
- I believe in you.
- I have time for you.
- I learn when I listen to you.
- This place is yours too.
- We need you here.

These affirmations are rooted in a belief that each child is fully worthy of respect simply because of his or her humanity. "Because you are a human being, endowed with the value and possibilities of humanity," believes the teacher, "I must treat you with dignity." Not only is dignity an unconditional entitlement of the child as a person, but it is also the gateway to self-esteem and, ultimately, to self-efficacy. Further, regard for the young person's humanity—complete with an ethic of caring—is essential to creating a community that models the way we ought to live together in the world (Beane, 1990; Sizer & Sizer, 1999).

FIGURE 3.1

The Teacher Responds

What Do the Elements Mean?

Invitation

- I have respect for who you are and who you can become.
- I want to know you.
- You are unique and valuable.
- I believe in you.
- I have time for you.
- I learn when I listen to you.
- This place is yours, too.
- We need you here.

Opportunity

- I have important things for you to do here today.
- The things I ask you to do are worthy things.
- The things I ask you to do are often daunting.
- The things I ask you to do open new possibilities for you.
- The things I give you to do here help you become all you can be.
- You have specific roles that make us all more efficient and effective.

Investment

- I work hard to make this place work for you.
- I work to make this place reflect you.
- I enjoy thinking about what we do here.
- I love to find new paths to success.
- It is my job to help you succeed.
- I am your partner in growth.
- I will do what it takes to ensure your growth.

Persistence

- You're growing, but you're not finished growing.
- When one route doesn't work, there are others we can find.
- Let's figure out what works best.
- There are no excuses here, but there is support.
- There is no finish line in learning.

Reflection

- I watch you and listen to you carefully and systematically.
- I make sure to use what I learn to help you learn better.
- I try to see things through your eyes.
- I continually ask, "How is this partnership working?"
- I continually, ask, "How can I make this better?"

With educational decision making grounded squarely in the dignity of each individual, the teacher's plans and actions radiate outward, and the implications of that core belief become evident:

> I have to get to know each child because I can accord each young person dignity only as I know and value the background, hopes, dreams, and fears of that particular individual. No child feels honored if he or she is seen as an interchangeable part—a widget like thousands of other widgets—a nameless entity with no identity outside the classroom and a sketchy one at best inside.

To know you, I must find many ways to listen to you and to learn about you. Even though I am dogged by the scarcity of time, I must help you sense that I have time for you.

Further, I must not only learn *about* you, I must learn *from* you. Unless the sharing enriches me, I will not be fed professionally or personally, and I will be less of a person and less of a professional than I could be. To learn to see the world through your eyes clarifies my own vision. If I study your culture, I am clearer about the influences that have shaped me. If I think about gender influences on your life, I understand more fully how gender has shaped me. If I understand your fears and dreams, my own stand in sharper relief. And, if I continually reflect on what you understand—or misunderstand—about what we are studying, I am sharper in grasping how meaning can be crafted through the content of the curriculum I teach.

I cannot accord you dignity unless I make you my partner in creating a classroom that mirrors the world we both want to live in. I must help you discover that you are unique and valuable among the group of us, even as I continue to guide you in reflecting on the uniqueness and value of each other member of the group. We must all come to believe in the huge potential each of us has to grow and develop— and actively support and celebrate that growth and development in every member of the classroom community. For the classroom to work, we must each be contributors to its success.

The classroom must be ours, not mine. The rules for living in the classroom must be our rules. The solutions to problems must be our solutions. The procedures we follow must come from a shared logic about how things need to work here for each of us to succeed.

The teacher's invitation—rooted in an unerring belief in the worth and dignity of each learner and multiplied to the classroom society that teacher and students will develop—becomes the catalyst for most of the decisions that will follow throughout the year. The teacher's invitation not only responds directly to the student's need for affirmation and contribution, but it also begins to respond to the student's need for power, purpose, and challenge.

First-year teacher Esmé Codell (1999) exemplifies invitation in many aspects of her work—even at the starting gate of teaching:

> In the morning, three things happen religiously. I say good morning real chipper to every single child and make sure they say good morning back. Then I collect "troubles" in a "Trouble Basket," a big green basket into which the children pantomime unburdening their home worries so they can concentrate on school. . . .This way, too, I can see what disposition the child is in when he or she enters. Finally, before the child can come in, they must give me a word, which I print on a piece of tagboard and they keep in an envelope. It can be any word, but preferably one that they heard and don't really know or one that is personally meaningful. . . .We go over the words when we do our private reading conferences. . . . It takes a long time to get in the door this way, but by the time we are in, I know every kid has had and given a kind greeting, has had an opportunity to learn, and has tried to leave his or her worries on the doorstep. Some kids from other classes sneak into our line to use the Trouble Basket or to get a word card (pp. 30–31).

The Response of Opportunity

If, as a teacher, my belief in you is unerring, and if I accord you the full dignity due human beings, I will do all I can to ensure that you will become all you should be. That means my goal will be to provide you maximum opportunity to develop your possibilities. To communicate that opportunity to students, the teacher's demeanor, words, and actions must continually say the following:

- I have important things for you to do here today.
- The things I ask you to do are worthy things.
- The things I ask you to do are often daunting.
- The things I ask you to do open new possibilities for you.
- The things I give you to do here help you become all you can be.
- You have specific roles here that make us all more efficient and effective.

Simply put, opportunity is more closely related to exhilaration than to drudgery. Genuine opportunity may be frightening, because it seems out of reach, but it is seldom stultifying. Opportunity requires hard work, but it is work with a purpose—it is work in pursuit of a dream. Said one science teacher who lives this philosophy, "We don't just keep them busy. We're giving them an opportunity" (Carter, 2001, p. 70).

To provide opportunity is to provide materials, tasks, applications, and problems that are rich with meaning for learners. To provide opportunity is to help learners *have* a voice in what and how they learn and to *find* their own voice through what they study. It is to feed the learner's curiosity and challenge the learner's natural drive toward competence (Meier, 1995).

Opportunity mandates that each child have a high-status education. That is,

each learner must be supported in gaining maximum access to and proficiency with the knowledge, ideas, and skills that open the doors to both present and future opportunity. Opportunity recognizes and extends as far as possible the potential of each individual to develop systems of knowledge and habits of thought and practice that typify successful, contributing adults.

Opportunity means enlivening the classroom. It means enlivening minds. It means creating for each learner the sorts of learning experiences we would have wished for ourselves and for our own children. In the end, opportunity is inclusive of each individual, fosters positive attitudes about self and learning, enhances meaning in both school and life, and engenders competence (Ginsberg & Wlodkowski, 2000).

Principal Helen DeBerry (Carter, 2001) explains what opportunity looks like in her Chicago school, where virtually all of the students are from minority and low-income homes and where student achievement is high: "All of our children are expected to work above grade level and to learn for the sake of learning. . . . We instill a desire to overachieve. Give us an average child and we'll make him an overachiever. Last year's 6th grade was reading *To Kill a Mockingbird*, while another class was writing its own stage play based on the story of the slave ship Amistad" (p. 55).

The Response of Investment

Perhaps the surest way for a teacher to communicate to learners that they are important individually and collectively and that their class work is compelling is for the teacher to model high investment in both the people and content of the classroom. The teacher who communicates investment to learners makes it clear:

- I work hard to make this place work for you.
- I work to make this place reflect you.
- I enjoy thinking about what we do here.
- I love to find new paths to success.
- It is my job to help you succeed.
- I am your partner in growth.
- I will do what it takes to ensure your growth.

Immersion in the classroom is evident in invested teachers. They give what it takes to make tomorrow's class work for everyone. Invested teachers are often the ones whose room contains students before school, at lunch, or after school. Students understand that the teacher has time for them and wants to provide both sanctuary and scaffolding for them.

Invested teachers share their thoughts about the classroom with their students. "Yesterday, I noticed some of you were having difficulty with the assignment you were working on," one teacher says as the day's class begins. "I thought about that last night and came up with a couple of new ways to think about the skills. I'll be interested in seeing what you think about the ideas." Beyond the words, the students hear, "We were on her mind last night. She cared enough about our success to give us her time even after we left. She means for us to succeed. She also wants our opinions."

Invested teachers make links with students' lives outside the classroom as well. Whether through making positive contacts with home, providing extracurricular activities, attending student events, or volunteering in the community, the invested teacher reaches out to know and support students in ways that extend what takes place in the classroom.

Invested teachers act as mentors for students, as advocates, and as partners (Beane, 1990; Ginsberg & Wlodkowski, 2000; Sizer & Sizer, 1999). These are roles that extend well beyond the roles of information provider and behavior manager. A mentor is one who works beside another to model important skills and sees to the success of the apprentice with those skills; a mentor makes it possible for individuals to take charge of their head and heart (Sizer & Sizer, 1999). An advocate is a voice in strong support of the individual—one who does what it takes to make certain the individual is heard and represented fairly. A partner is one who not only "acts for people (on their behalf) as 'objects of our care,' but also *with* them, as mutual 'subjects' in the human experience" (Beane, 1990, p. 62).

Finally, invested teachers are personally engaged in what they ask the students to do. That is, invested teachers work hard at learning, spend free time in pursuit of knowledge, think and puzzle over problems, and get excited about ideas. Invested teachers have clear personal goals toward which they work steadily. Invested teachers exemplify the pursuit of excellence:

> There are positive examples that tell their own story. The biology teacher

who, spring after spring, tracks the nesting patterns of red-winged blackbirds, dragging his students before dawn into a mosquito-infested swamp to watch and record the movements of the birds. The English teacher who writes poetry and shares it with her students, and not only teaches drama, but directs student performances. The coach who keeps on top of her game, razor-sharp on new rules, plays, and practices and always ready to share them. The custodian who in his work exhibits pride of place and insistently, politely, and persuasively expects students to do likewise. The assistant principal who makes certain he learns the name of every student within a month of the opening of school and who greets and treats each student with knowing familiarity (Sizer & Sizer, 1999, p. 11).

These educators communicate investment. Students do not miss the message. These are teachers invested in what they teach, whom they teach, and where they teach, and the ideals for which they stand. Their messages come not simply from slogans on classroom walls, but from living out their beliefs.

The Response of Persistence

Classrooms are messy with agendas, complex material, and imperfect lives. Procedures designed to make the day go smoothly don't always work the first time—or the fourth. Students don't always grasp ideas on carefully prescribed timetables. Young people are as likely to resist challenge as to embrace it. The teacher needs to help students understand that this is a place where persistence is a hallmark. To do that, the teacher must communicate the following:

- You're growing, but you're not finished growing.

- When one route doesn't work, there are others we can find.
- Let's figure out what works best.
- There are no excuses here, but there is support.
- There is no finish line in learning.

The teacher who genuinely believes in the possibilities of each individual is not easily discouraged. That teacher does not question the educability of any student—race, class, and prior experience notwithstanding (Ayres, Klonsky, & Lyon, 2000). *Different* is not a synonym for *deficient* (Finnan & Swanson, 2000). Although the persistent teacher understands the internal and external impediments to learning faced by nearly every student, even the most able, that teacher recognizes no excuses for inferior work. Instead, there is a predictable support system for moving forward. When a student is "missing the mark," the persistent teacher does not assume the student *cannot* learn, but rather assumes the student *is* not learning in the way he is currently being taught. The persistent teacher will find another way. In the eyes of that teacher, when a student fails, the teacher fails (Carter, 2001).

I recently met a retired teacher, now in her late seventies. Hearing that I was in her town to work with teachers on "differentiation," she asked for an explanation of what the term meant. As I tried to encapsulate the meaning of the concept, her eyes sparked. "Oh, I know what you mean," she said and smiled broadly. "When I taught young children, I developed five or six different ways to teach the skills of reading. I just tried different approaches with different children, until I found out the one that worked for that child. If none of the approaches I'd used in the past worked, I developed another way." She continued, "Later, I taught English. I found that some students learned grammar best by diagramming sentences, some by transactional grammar, and some by analyzing signs on the streets and in magazines. There was always a way that would work, if I just kept looking." That's persistence in search of success!

The persistent teacher also models the steady but relentless quest for excellence. The persistent teacher generously acknowledges the distance a student has come academically, but also makes clear the distance each student has yet to go. That teacher helps students realize that the quest for quality never ends. If the quest ends, quality ends with it—and so does the growth of the individual.

The persistent teacher not only points out that learning has no finish line for students, but lives according to that principle as well. That teacher fights "success ego," never succumbing to the sense that she is "good enough" to be exempt from the need to change. "We're all on a journey," the persistent teacher believes, "none of us is ever through striving."

The Response of Reflection

Reflective practice is important, because effective teaching defies any set of "rules for practice." There is no formula for success. Rather, we work in "indeterminate zones of practice" (Schon, 1987), where uncertainty, ambiguity, and uniqueness are key constants in the teacher's world. Indeed, if we accept the premise of the dignity of the individual, recognize the diversity that implies, and combine that with the need to honor the group as well as the individual, we have already entered an indeterminate zone.

From the film *Apollo 13*, two powerful moments endure. The first comes when astronauts far away from the earth signal back to ground command, "Houston, we have a problem." The second follows when the commander of operations in Houston pulls together a team of experts with varied specialties, outlines the critical nature of their role in trying to save the lives of the astronauts, and concludes with the statement, "Failure is not an option."

Given the nature of the classroom and its inhabitants, young lives are always at risk. There is always a problem. The teacher who believes deeply in the dignity and worth of the individual and the group hears the echo, "Failure is not an option."

The nature of schools is such that teachers must continually address critical problems, serving largely as an expert "team of one." Wise teachers expand their team in a variety of ways—forming partnerships with their students, establishing relationships with like-minded peers who serve as "critical friends," drawing on the expertise of specialists in the building, and actively pursuing advanced professional knowledge through universities, books, and high-quality staff development. Still, by and large teacher expertise develops in proportion to teacher reflection on practice.

Not only do teachers benefit from reflective practice, but students derive important messages from reflective teachers as well. To the student, a reflective teacher communicates the following:

- I watch you and listen to you carefully and systematically.
- I make sure to use what I learn to help you learn better.
- I try to see things through your eyes.
- I continually ask, "How is this partnership working?"
- "I continually ask, "How can I make this better?"

The reflective teacher questions not only daily practice but also beliefs that should ground that practice. To what degree am I living my beliefs? In what ways does this place dignify or diminish each individual? To what degree am I an example of the kind of learner and person I ask my students to be? To what extent does this class commend the value of diversity in background, opinion, and talent? Am I aiming for a norm or for the best each child has to offer? What do I understand about the differences among people? What do I understand about the things all humans share in common? To what degree does this community we call a classroom help its inhabitants know how to live more effectively with other people? How well does this microworld equip young people for life in the greater world?

To answer these questions, of course, the teacher also reflects on the details of classroom practice. How well am I monitoring student readiness to learn and learning progress? How effectively am I using what I learn from assessment to guide lesson planning and teaching? What else do I need to know about my students' interests and modes of learning? How can I best build a three-dimensional portrait of each learner? At what points are classroom routines clear to everyone, and when do they help us work more effectively? When do they fail us in one way or another? What changes ought I to make in daily details that contribute to the greater goals of the classroom?

Teacher reflection inevitably attends directly to students' need for affirmation, contribution, power, purpose, and challenge. From continual reflection on these and countless other questions, the teacher's practice also becomes ever more intuitive and efficient in addressing student needs. Reflection also supports what Deborah Meier (1995) calls the power to care. It may well be that one of the factors that overwhelms our early visions of the possibilities in classrooms is encountering so many human needs at the very time we are so ill equipped to address them. Feeling such personal inadequacy may compel us to stop looking at the needs—to build a protective wall between the hurt of the young and our disappointment in ourselves.

> There is a terrible and pointless pain in powerless caring, and it erodes the capacity for caring. . . .We needed time and again to discover ways to effectively care. Part of it depended on having sufficient power. We kept extensive notes and records of children's work, continuously experimenting with better ways to keep and use such information. We met to work out ways to sharpen our observational skill at understanding children's learning

modes and preferences as individuals—what engaged them most deeply, how they responded best to criticism. . . . We worked together to better organize curriculum as well as increase our knowledge about the subjects that our students were studying. . . . We attended all manner of courses and institutes that suited our interests and needs. Being seen as intellectually curious people, modeling what a mathematician, historian, or scientist does, are rock-bottom necessities if kids are to catch on to what we're teaching about. Our desire to teach, after all, needs to be connected always to our enthusiasm and respect for what (and who) we are teaching about (Meier, 1995, p. 133–134).

The Devil Lurks in the Translation

In the musings of this chapter and the previous one, it should be becoming more evident that "differentiated" teaching seems an imperative if we accept the teacher's role in connecting with students. How could we issue an invitation to the risky endeavor of learning if it is a mass-produced invitation? How could we dignify a learner without offering that learner things to do that are important enough to give roots and wings to his or her dreams? How could we learn about the needs of the individual student or attend to those needs without full investment? How could we make it all work for such varied individuals without dogged persistence? How would we find our way and help our students find their individual paths without deep reflection?

It is circular. To establish ties with a student, we must (as the fox explains in *The Little Prince*) come to see how each student is unlike every other—and to see that, we must form ties with that student.

On some level, it's not so difficult to accept that circular premise. Most of us as teachers mean to see and honor the individual. As always, the devil is in the details. How do we translate abstract ideas into the very daily stuff of classroom life? What do tomorrow's lesson plans have to do with dignity, diversity, and democracy (Beane, 1990)? Chapter 4 will explore ways in which the concrete decisions we make about classroom operation translate into teacher response to learner needs—how those decisions lay the groundwork for thinking about curriculum and instruction.

4

Teacher Response to Student Needs: Rationale to Practice

"Charlie," he said, "do you know why I gave you all that extra work?"

I shook my head no. That look on his face. It made me quiet.

"Charlie, do you know how smart you are?"

I just shook my head no again . . . .

"Charlie, you're one of the most gifted people I've ever known. And I don't mean in terms of my other students. I mean in terms of anyone I've ever met. That's why I gave you the extra work . . . . I'm not trying to make you feel uncomfortable. I just want you to know you're very special . . . and the only reason I'm telling you this is that I don't know if anyone else ever has . . . . So when the school year ends, and I'm not your teacher any more, I want you to know that if you ever need anything, or want to know more about books, or want to show me anything you write, you can always come to me as a friend. I do consider you a friend, Charlie."

I didn't say anything for a while because I didn't know what to say. So finally I just said, "You're the best teacher I've ever had" (Chbosky, 1999, pp. 181–182).

Fox-taming teachers who seek to establish a classroom with an eye to forming ties with students begin the process with a particular sort of latitude and longitude that will serve as a navigation guide for their professional decision making. By accepting every student's need for affirmation, contribution, power, purpose, and challenge, the teacher intends to provide invitation and opportunity for each student through investment, persistence, and reflection. There is now a line of logic to govern the teacher's thought and action. Both covertly and overtly, the teacher lets learners know the following:

- You are unique and valuable as individuals, and we are important as a class.
- We are here to help you find and develop abilities as individuals and as a class.
- Our goal is to help each person and our class become as capable as possible.

- That is an important goal, and the work we do to achieve it must be both important and challenging.
- The time we have to achieve our goal is valuable.
- Therefore, we have to figure out together how to work in the most effective and efficient ways we can.
- We'll need to learn about one another and ourselves, so we know where we need to go and how we're doing in getting there.
- We'll need to determine guidelines for working, so we can reach our goal, both individually and as a class.
- We'll need to figure out working routines that enable us to succeed in reaching our goals, both individually and as a class.
- We'll need to develop support systems to ensure that we continually grow, both individually and as a class.
- Like all important goals, our goal will require investment and persistence.

The teacher also conveys these overarching messages: "You'll see those things in me as your teacher. I'll expect to see them in you as individuals and in our class as a whole. I need you to join me in making our class work for each of us." Guided by this map of thought, the teacher weighs decisions and actions. Each element of the classroom takes its shape from this progression of thought—for both teacher and students. Classroom environment, classroom communication, class guidelines, working routines, support systems, and shared responsibility are molded according to the roles they must play in achieving the goal of maxi-

mizing the growth and capacity of each individual learner and of the class as a group. Investment, persistence, and reflection fuel the journey.

In this chapter, we'll look at how classroom elements and attributes derive their form from when teachers respond proactively and concretely to learner needs. In each instance, we'll review the roles of the element or attribute in teaching and learning, share scenarios of classrooms in action, and provide a few examples of translating the element or attribute into the classroom.

The Classroom Environment

The classroom environment includes both physical and affective attributes that individually and cumulatively establish the tone or atmosphere in which teaching and learning will take place. From the first day of a class until the last, environment will quietly but potently form a line of communication from teacher to student, student to student, and student to teacher. Environment will support or deter the student's quest for affirmation, contribution, power, purpose, and challenge in the classroom. Environment also will speak to the presence or absence of invitation and opportunity to each child individually and, ultimately, to the class as a whole. It will often be the first messenger of how learning will be in this place.

Walls, bulletin boards, and artifacts reveal much about the wonder or sterility of learning. Furniture arrangement speaks of partnership or isolation, of flexibility or standardization. Materials represent the presence or absence of interest in varied cultures, languages, talents, learning needs, and dreams. Exhibits, learning tools, charts, and posters suggest a place where help is a given. Their absence suggests otherwise. What a student sees in the classroom implies the centrality of the student—or of the teacher.

Just as the teacher is primary architect of the physical attributes of the classroom, so he or she initiates the affective climate of the classroom. Does the teacher find a way to speak to students individually, or is the teacher too busy with other things that must be more important? Is there excitement in the way the teacher addresses individual learners and the class, or does voice tone suggest a prerecorded event? Is humor positive and energizing, or does it diminish individuals in some way? Does the teacher's demeanor reflect unequivocal respect for each learner, or is it pretty clear who is favored in some way?

Environment communicates loudly, if subtly, about personal affirmation, potential for individual contribution, power derived from knowledge, purposefulness of the learning enterprise, and high challenge. It signals students daily about ways in which their uniqueness is recognized and valued—or signals to them that they are replaceable and interchangeable parts in an impersonal machine.

Scenarios of Environmental Decisions in the Classroom

Critical in the early years of schooling, learning environment is no less so as students move through the elementary, middle, high school, and college years. In each new developmental stage, we must find our way—find ourselves—all over again. Learning environment remains key in that process.

Scenario 1. Ms. Narvez carefully plans the "geography" of her elementary classroom. She has three important goals that guide this part of her environmental planning. First, she wants students to "see themselves" in the room. Second, she wants the room to convey a message of flexibility. Third, she wants students to begin to understand that the work they do is important and interesting as they view the room.

To ensure that students "see themselves" in the room, she makes certain that featured books and posters represent students from a wide range of cultures and backgrounds. She also has an active and changing "Kids' Corner" that contains artifacts likely to be intriguing to students. Sometimes she places artifacts in the Kids' Corner to encourage students to examine useful tools, solve relevant problems, or try out varied approaches. Students regularly bring in artifacts they think are interesting. These may reflect their own interests or something they are studying.

To help convey the message of flexibility, Ms. Narvez uses varied kinds of furniture: tables of different shapes and sizes, desks, carrels for quiet work; a sharing area that features pillows and rug squares so that students can read and write in small groups; and floor space where students can sit as a class for informal planning and sharing sessions. To help students sense that their work is important, the teacher has a large bulletin board labeled "Working with the Experts." The board has two sections. In the left side, she and the students place articles about adults who write, work with math, figure out the puzzles of history, and so on. Students also contribute letters they receive or interview excerpts from adults they've contacted as they work on projects. On the right of the board are examples of student work that have some hallmarks of real-world quality: the work may have been developed to solve a real-life problem, to help an audience outside the classroom, to teach someone, and so on. There are also shelves under the bulletin board that hold three-dimensional artifacts representing the work of both professionals and students. Ms. Narvez often leads students in talking about how their work is like that of the professionals as well as ways in which they can learn from the professionals how to keep growing.

Scenario 2. Mr. Atcheson is keenly aware of his role in establishing a positive environment in his high school classroom. There are a number of practices to which he regularly attends. He is always at the door as students enter and leave the room. This is one way he can make personal contact with the very large number of students he teaches. He finds that the personal contact helps him connect with and understand the students better over time, and it helps them "settle in" for class. He also makes certain he calls on students equitably. He works hard to ensure that he calls on males and females equally, that he calls on students from all cultural groups with the same frequency, and that he consistently calls

on students of varying readiness levels. He wants the students to know he needs and expects each of them to contribute to the success of the class.

Mr. Atcheson also uses a system he calls "One and One" to hear and attend to student opinions and feelings. Every two or three weeks, he gives students an index card near the end of class. He asks students to use one side of the card to tell him how class is going for them. He encourages them to write what's going well, what's not going well, and suggestions for making the class more effective. On the other side of the card, he asks students to tell him something about themselves that they think would be useful or interesting to him. He reminds the students that he's a better teacher when he knows them better. They can provide the name of a book they're reading, how their soccer team is doing, what songs they're enjoying listening to, something they've accomplished that they're pleased with, and so on. He uses class-related information to shape his instruction, and lets the students know as he does so. He uses student-related information to enable him to build bridges of conversation with individuals in the moments he can find to connect with them during work time in class, as they come and go in the classroom, and as he sees them in the hall.

Finally, in class discussions, Mr. Atcheson regularly encourages students to share varied perspectives on issues and topics they discuss. He reminds students that they are all better informed and better thinkers if they understand both their own positions and those of people who see things differently. He uses the varied perspectives to talk about the richness that comes from having students with different experiences in the classroom.

Scenario 3. Ms. Timmons understands that both teacher and student talk greatly affect the tone of the classroom. For that reason, she teaches her middle schoolers how to listen respectfully to the ideas of peers, how to make suggestions that are positive in tone, how to build on one another's ideas, and how to debate ideas in ways that are respectful of both the ideas and the people who hold them. She is consistent in modeling these attributes as well. She also talks often about how important errors can be in helping us understand our thinking better. She's willing to share with students her own imperfections and how she learns daily from things that go well and those that don't. Ms. Timmons is also purposeful in her use of humor in the classroom. Her students enjoy her quick wit, and she enjoys their own sense of humor. With her own example and guidance, she makes certain that humor is used "to make us better," not to "make us hurt." She finds that positive humor can regularly defuse tense situations in class and has long since learned that sarcasm has no place in positive environments.

Additional Strategies to Build Positive Environments

These examples of actions teachers can take to help create a positive learning environment are just a few of the concrete ways of contributing to such settings. A few more ideas and strategies follow.

Study Students' Cultures. Work consistently to become familiar with students' cultures, languages, and neighborhoods. What is valued in the student's world? What family roles and relationships matter? What are important celebrations? How does the grammar of the language ' work for students whose first language is not English? Each new insight holds clues to make teaching more responsive and learning more compelling.

Convey Status. Elizabeth Cohen (1994) points to the need to find individual students doing important and worthwhile things in the classroom and to share these insights with the students' peers. Cohen cautions that such comments from the teacher must be natural and honest, not contrived and manipulated. Under those conditions, she points out, teachers can help students see one another as significant contributors to the success of the group. Although this is important for all learners, conveying status is particularly effective in helping students see the possibilities in peers who are quiet, who have backgrounds different from the majority, or who struggle with learning. In the end, teachers need to commend each student in legitimate ways, and show how valuable each one is to the work of the group.

Commend Creativity. When there are many materials students can use to explore or express learning, a tone of possibility results. When a room contains color, interesting things to look at, and evidence of the personality of teacher, students, and class as a whole, there is a sense that many kinds of people make contributions to the room.

Make Room for All Kinds of Learners. A classroom that has space for students who need quiet as well as for those who need interaction is a more positive place for more students than one that provides for only one of those needs. A classroom that manifests hands-on learning experiences as well as written and spoken approaches to learning is friendlier to a larger number of students (for more information, see Clayton & Forton, 2001).

Help Students Know About One Another. Some teachers use interest groups, shared-interest reading, or both as a way for students to find peers who enjoy similar topics or approaches to learning. Balancing similar-interest groups with groups deliberately composed to reflect an array of interests could further extend student thinking and appreciation of peers. "Word Jars," "Idea Jars," or "Question Boxes" are useful in helping students hear from one another. In these containers, students place new words they are discovering, new ideas they are developing, or questions about which they are wondering. Teachers can draw from these to develop classroom discussions or tasks, or just to invite students to contribute their thinking in transitional times in the classrooms.

"Morning Meetings" also can be a consistent means of helping students get to know one another and of building community throughout the year. These daily sessions often include greetings, sharing, a group activity, and announcements. They set a positive tone at the outset of the day, help students feel safe and welcomed, teach routines, foster positive communications, and allow opportunities for students to share ideas (Kriete, 2002).

Celebrate Success. One teacher made it a point to call the parents of several students each week to share something positive that had taken place with their child in the classroom during the previous week. The call might focus on a student who was able to comfortably use a particular skill for the first time, a very bright learner who was beginning to accept challenge, a student who helped another student in a significant way, and so on. Another teacher e-mailed some of his secondary students each week with comments about positives in their work, contributions to class, and so on. Still another teacher brought to the classroom a giant bowl of old keys of many kinds. She gave each learner a key ring. When any learner had an important breakthrough in the classroom (such as asking a really pivotal and insightful question, challenging herself in a genuinely noteworthy way, attaining a new level of competence in an area) the student selected a key to place on her ring. The fact that every child in the class could tell visitors or peers exactly what each key represented spoke of the importance to them of having benchmarks in their development noted and celebrated.

As this chapter examines communications, guidelines, routines, support systems, and shared leadership, you'll see that most of the strategies in those categories also contribute to a positive classroom environment. You'll note also that a strategy in any one category is likely to overlap with other categories.

The more fundamental and concrete suggestions in this section simply lay a foundation for a whole array of additional ways to respond to the student's need for affirmation, contribution, power, purpose, and challenge.

Communication in the Classroom

Early and fundamental decisions about classroom environment certainly address and affect communication in the classroom. However, there is a broad array of specific strategies for ensuring that teachers and students communicate effectively and efficiently, that communication improves learning, and that everyone in the class shares an evolving understanding of why the classroom operates as it does. Among the roles communications patterns in the classroom can play are

- Building a group identity,
- Ensuring that the teacher has ways of getting to know students better,
- Enabling the teacher to share his or her thinking about teaching, and
- Providing a shorthand for quick communication among members of the classroom community.

Scenarios of Communications Decisions in the Classroom

Teachers can build positive and productive classroom communications patterns with various approaches and strategies.

Scenario 1. Mr. Engle makes it a point to teach metacognitively. That is, he explains to his students the thinking behind his decisions and plans. For example, he might say, "Last night, I was looking at your learning log entries and found out that there are two important places in your thinking where there is still some fuzz. So today, I'm going to give you some work to do that will target the particular need you have at this point." At another time he might say, "I wasn't quite comfortable with the way class ended yesterday. I did some thinking about it afterward and I have some thoughts about how we might make things smoother for all of us, but first, I'd really like to hear your ideas." This sort of metacognitive teaching, he finds, helps students understand that he invests time and energy in making the class effective. It also assures them that his dealings with them are reasoned and purposeful rather than arbitrary. Further, it allows him to model for his students the kind of thinking he wants them to do about their own work and invites them to join him in thinking about how to make the class excellent.

Scenario 2. Ms. Ames builds communications throughout the year to help her students understand their similarities and differences and to guide them in developing a sense of community. She has students complete personal profiles that help her understand how they see their particular strengths (see Toolbox, Figures T.1 and T.2 for suggested student surveys). She graphs or otherwise displays the results and leads students in thinking about what kind of classroom they'd need to help everyone build strengths, support growth in weaker areas, expand current interests, discover new interests, and learn in effective ways.

These early discussions set the foundation for many that follow, as students and teacher establish goals, guidelines, and routines for the class and assess their progress in those areas. The same profiles help Ms. Ames begin an ongoing conversation about strengths that individual students bring to the group and class tasks. Early on, the profile sheets help establish work groups in which each member can contribute and through which each member is likely to be challenged. As the year continues, students review, revise, and extend portions of their surveys to reflect change and growth.

Scenario 3. Ms. Callison and her students developed a shorthand phrase for striving for one's best work. The phrase is "working for a bingo." When she asks students if a particular piece of work is a bingo, they know an affirmative answer means she'll find the student has done everything he could to achieve excellence. The phrase has become part of the identity of the class.

Scenario 4. Ms. Marquissee and her students have also developed a shared communication shorthand. When a student does something noteworthy, the teacher will say, "Pat your brain!" As the year goes on, students use this shorthand with each other and themselves. She also does "windshield checks" with her students. Following a discussion or presentation, she ask students if their windshields are clear, have a few bugs stuck to them, or are covered with mud. She provides subsequent activities to help clarify and extend student proficiency based on the windshield check. Sometimes, individual students will say to her, "Ms. Marquissee,

I have a mud problem. Can you help me?" or "My windshield is really clear. Can I move on?" (Brimijoin, Marquissee, & Tomlinson, 2003)

Scenario 5. Similarly, Mr. Lucas and his students know what it means to "diversi*fy*" (provide more than one perspective), "veri*fy*" (offer proof or evidence), and "ampli*fy*" (elaborate on an idea). Not only does he use these three terms as shorthand to challenge students in discussions and assignments, but his students learn to use the terms as a measure of their own thinking and that of writers and speakers they encounter. A person whose thinking is fully developed and thus includes all three terms is a "Fy^3."

Scenario 6. Ms. Jones allows students to work in the biology room during lunch. The energy level in the room is great as students talk with one another and the teacher about their ideas, questions, and projects. There is an evident sense of community among teacher and students who populate the room during lunch, as well as a palpable sense of excitement about science. In a crowded day, the presence of students in the teacher's room at lunch costs Ms. Jones some "peace and quiet." The payoff for the cost has been much better teacher-student and student-student communication and more student buy-in to the curriculum.

Additional Strategies to Foster Positive Communication

These scenarios provide concrete examples of ways in which teachers promote effective communication. Some additional avenues to communication that foster a positive learning environment follow.

Hold Goal-Setting Conferences. In goal-setting conferences, a teacher meets with one student to talk about that student's progress in a particular area or perspectives on a particular project. Together, they examine some of the student's work, talk about strengths and next steps, and set goals (with a heavy emphasis on student input) for a prescribed time period. Goal-setting conferences allow for one-on-one exchanges that are difficult to come by in busy classrooms. They also foster student understanding and ownership of their own learning.

Use Dialogue Journals. Dialogue journals are designed solely for the purpose of allowing student and teacher to "talk" in ways that often are not possible during class. Teachers who use dialogue journals generally ask students to write in them two or three times early in the year. Entries can be about anything the student would like to tell or ask the teacher about—music, sports preferences, favorite movies or books, and so on. Once students are familiar with the dialogue journals, they write in them when they like to and sometimes when the teacher asks the class as a whole to share opinions on a particular topic. A teacher may also initiate a dialogue journal entry for a particular student. Dialogue journals may be paper or electronic.

Incorporate Teacher Talk Groups in Lesson Plans. When students are working individually or in small groups, a teacher announces the names of students with whom she would like to meet, generally in groups of three to five. Group membership varies continually. "Teacher talk" groups usually meet for about 5 minutes. During these sessions, the teacher is able to check for student understanding of content, skills, assignment directions, and group functioning. It's sort of a "dip stick" assessment that not only helps the teacher understand individual needs more fully, but also yields a sense of how the class is functioning. Also, many students talk more freely in these small groups than in whole class exchanges.

Guidelines for Classroom Operation

Learners are adaptable. It's likely that most of them can adapt to varied sets of rules or guidelines most of the time. It's important, of course, that the learners are clear on what the guidelines are and why they exist. Classroom guidelines are generally best conceived not as arbitrary rules recorded on paper, distributed to students, and discussed on the first day of class, but as agreements forged to ensure a classroom that supports maximum success for each of its learners. It's also likely that a few thoughtful guidelines are more potent than a long list of more trivial ones, especially if the guidelines are positive in tone. There will still be a need to communicate what students can do if they don't have a pencil, or under what circumstances a student can go to the restroom. However, it's useful to realize, and help students realize, that decisions regarding these details are governed by the few essential classroom guidelines.

The wording of the guidelines will vary with the age of the student, but great classrooms can grow from four general rules:

1. We will show respect for people, their ideas, and their property.
2. We will work hard to ensure our own growth and to assist the growth of others.
3. We will persist, even when things are difficult and uncertain.
4. We will accept responsibility for the quality of our work and for our behaviors and actions.

Certainly, different teachers and classes would conceive what's essential in somewhat different ways and express their intent in somewhat different language.

In any case, guidelines should focus on helping students understand and articulate that the class will be governed by "what we need to succeed." If a community of learners could live according to respect, hard work, persistence, and responsibility, the chances would be high that each student could find in that classroom affirmation, contribution, power, purpose, and challenge.

Scenarios of Guidelines for Operation in the Classroom

There are other "beliefs we live by" that help teachers and students establish a positive and productive tone. Students and teachers together shape the principles that will guide their time with each other as a community of learners.

Scenario 1. Ms. Gandy communicates early and often to her primary students that she gets excited when a student grows, and that she hopes they will, too. She will sometimes stop the class when students are working independently or in groups and ask them to gather with her around the desk or work area of someone in the class. She invites the student in question to explain what he has just successfully done. "Could you do that last week?" she asks. When the student says no, she exclaims to the class, "Isn't that great? Shawn grew!" Her students come to understand that a central premise in their classroom is that individual growth is a big deal and should be celebrated. Over time, students begin to focus more on individual growth than competition. That has much to do with students affirming one another, accepting responsibility for their own work, and thinking about grades in a redemptive way.

Scenario 2. Ms. Rex and her students talk about "X-Factor" efforts. A student does X-Factor work when she goes well beyond what was required for "quality" work. In other words, the student has really pushed herself to an unexpected level. Students and teacher also developed a language for gradations of quality in their work. They understand that X-Factor work is not an everyday occurrence. They also understand that if they strive to be X-Factor learners, they will go further in their learning than if they settle for "getting by" (Kiernan, 2002).

Scenario 3. Mr. Francisco helps his math students cultivate the habit of "trying three different ways" before giving up or asking for help. He frequently asks for an explanation of the three ways a student has tried to solve a problem before he kicks in with an explanation. He asks students to do the same with one another. This guideline not only helps students accept responsibility for their own work, but also increases the likelihood that they are actively reasoning as they work.

Scenario 4. Ms. Kopinski works with her high school students to delineate what it means to be a colleague. They talk about collegiality in varied walks of life. How might an actor be a good colleague? Or an athlete? Or a musical group member? They arrive at a sense of how one can be supportive of the needs of others and what we do (intentionally or unintentionally) that undercuts the growth and opportunities of colleagues. The conversation continues in brief spurts throughout the year and becomes a centerpiece for teacher and student thought about what a high school community of learners should look like and how it should operate.

Scenario 5. At An Achievable Dream Academy in Newport News, Virginia, students have binders that designate their grade level. Each student must keep a continual record of assignments, their status, and resulting grades in his binder. The schedules and binders must be ready for inspection and discussion at any time. This is one of *many* ways the unique school helps students take responsibility for their own learning.

Additional Strategies to Enhance Classroom Operation

There are countless strategies that signal to students both intent for effective classroom guidelines and ways to help achieve them. Here are a few additional such strategies.

Time is Valuable. Let students know you want them to work with you to become good stewards of time. Use spare moments wisely and let students know how to do that as well. Anchor activities, or tasks to which students automatically move as soon as they complete an assignment, are one good way to help students cultivate the habit of using time wisely and with a clear purpose (see Toolbox, Figure T.3).

Fair is Ensuring All Learners Get What They Need to Succeed. In many classrooms, "fair" means making sure that everyone is treated exactly the same way. That turns out to be a counterproductive approach for students who are far ahead in their work, who struggle with their work, who learn in nontraditional ways, who are from diverse cultural groups, who come from low-income homes, and so on. It's more productive to think about crafting a classroom in which people work toward making sure each person gets what he or she needs to grow and develop as fully as possible.

Teach Up, Work Up. When a teacher intentionally pitches the curriculum a bit beyond the point he believes students can reach, the results can be quite dramatic. When students learn to accept and ultimately embrace challenge, they become much stronger individuals. Classrooms in which students come to realize that the teacher teaches for intellectual challenge and come to enjoy meeting that challenge are dynamic places for everyone involved. (Later in the chapter, we'll look at some of the support systems teachers and students can develop to promote success at a high level of intellectual challenge.)

Classroom Routines

Classrooms in which there is enough flexibility to reach out to students with varied learning needs are paradoxical in that they derive much of their flexibility from routine. In fact, clear and predictable classroom routines are probably the difference between productivity and chaos for classrooms where teachers attempt to address variations among learners.

In such classrooms, students have to develop a high degree of successful autonomy. After all, the teacher will not be available to all students all the time to reiterate directions, guide efficient movement around the room, give reminders about time, and so on. That students should develop autonomy as learners ought to be a primary goal of all classrooms from preschool onward. Failure to ensure that students become progressively more independent learners constitutes educational malpractice. Nonetheless, it is difficult to teach the skills of autonomy when there are 25 to 40 young bodies in a room. As a result, many of us become more skilled at doing things for our students than at teaching them to do those things for themselves. So long as we teach as though "the students" were one student, we can get by with enabling student dependence. As soon as we set out to deal proactively with students as individuals, we must become more adept at helping students help themselves.

If we subscribe to the uniqueness of the individual and intend to make affirmation, contribution, power, purpose, and challenge happen for individuals, we must become skilled at building routines that take us out of the business of pulling puppet strings on a moment-by-moment basis in the classroom. Routines ensure that students understand how the class will begin and end, how to get and put away materials, how to keep records of their work, how to move around the classroom in acceptable ways, how to use time wisely, how to figure out where they should be and what they should be doing at a given time, where to put work when they finish, how to get help when the teacher is working directly with others, and so on. Not only are teachers more able to support affirmation, contribution, power, purpose, and challenge when students adhere to effective and efficient routines, but students themselves also achieve a great deal of those five elements from classrooms that continually escalate their capacity for independence.

Scenarios of Routines in Flexible Classrooms

Teachers develop effective classroom routines in many ways. The routines both reflect and serve the nature and needs of the teacher and students. The goal of such routines is to facilitate individual learning and shared community.

Scenario 1. Ms. Schlim created four room-arrangement charts and posted them on a classroom bulletin board. Each had a different name: seminar format, discussion format, small-group format, and team format. As the year began, she made sure the students knew how to move furniture quietly and quickly and how furniture should be arranged for each of the four configurations. Within a short time, she could say to her students,

"Please rearrange the room in the seminar format." Within a matter of seconds, each student would move one or two pieces of furniture to its new position and would be seated and ready to work as well. In a secondary classroom with only armchair desks, this gave the teacher and her students much more flexibility in working options. The fact that students knew how to move the furniture efficiently made her much more willing to be flexible than when she felt she had to move the furniture herself.

Scenario 2. Mr. Kahlim's students know that when they enter his room in the morning, they should place their homework in the red basket by the door. They then go to the book bins and select a book to read silently or with a friend. Shared reading takes place on the side of the room near the teacher's desk. Silent reading takes place on the side of the room near the windows. When it's time for the day to begin officially, the teacher turns on some music. That is the signal for students to put away their materials and join him in the front of the room. They know to sit "squared off" (facing the teacher) and "eyes up" (ready to make eye contact). The day begins with students sharing something interesting from home or from their reading, contributing a personal goal for the day, and examining the wall chart that gives students their initial work and location in the room (see Toolbox, Figure T.4). Students ask questions about their tasks and have 30 seconds to be working productively in their assigned places. The predictability of the start to the day provides autonomy within structure and

reinforces a sense of community, clarity of purpose, and individual responsibility.

Scenario 3. Ms. Alexander uses four routines to ensure that students have access to help when they need it while she is working with individuals or a small group of students. First, she reminds students to "raise their antennae" when she gives directions. This shorthand reminds students to listen carefully and ask questions at that point, because she will soon be off limits. Second, she often appoints one or more "consultants" for a specified time span or task. These students wear a cap or cardboard tag designating their role. They are available to answer questions about directions or work.

Students also use "stop and go" cards. When a student is working confidently, the green "go" side of the index card is facing up on the desk. That signals to the teacher that the student is doing fine. When a student feels uncertain and would like help from the teacher, the red "stop" side of the card faces up. Of course the teacher checks with all students as she can, but the signals help her give support efficiently when she leaves work with a small group or individual and begins circulating through the class.

Finally, Ms. Alexander uses a "Red Cross Emergency" system for getting help. Every student has a tongue depressor with their name on it in a green can. Beside the green can is a white can with a large red cross on it. When students need "emergency help," they take their tongue depressors out of the green can and place them in the "Red Cross Emergency" can. Ms. Alexander looks here first when she begins to circulate among students as they work. She also keeps her eye on the Red Cross Emergency can as she works with small groups or individuals so that she is quickly aware of students who are feeling really stuck despite other options for assistance.

Additional Classroom Routines That Support Flexible Teaching

There are many routines that ultimately enhance the ability of students to grow and learn.

Use Visual Cues. Signs posted strategically around the classroom can help students remember where to put work, steps to follow at a given work station, how to record completed work, where they are in the class schedule, and so on. Icons or particular colors plus words can make signs useful to students who are not yet fluent readers—including students learning English. A designated sound or a hand signal combined with a teacher's voice can remind students that they need to speak more softly, bring work to completion, switch tasks, and so on.

Pre-establish Groups. At the beginning of a unit, a teacher may want to plan for students to be in several sorts of groups in the weeks ahead. Rather than stopping to form and announce groups at multiple points in the day, the teacher may designate several group formations at the outset of the unit. One student may be a member of four or five groups. The groups are sometimes named for times (9 O'clock Group, 11 O'clock Group, etc.) The names do not suggest that a student will necessarily meet with a 9 O'clock Group at 9:00. Rather, they are simply a procedural way for establish-

ing groups quickly. The groups can have more descriptive names, for example: Think Tanks (problem-solving groups), Review Groups (heterogeneous), Challenge Groups (homogeneous based on recent assessments), and Task Forces (product groups). The teacher provides all students with a list of their individual groups and names as the unit begins. The lists can also be posted. Students may contribute their own preferences for partners in one or more of the groups based on shared interests or effective working relationships. Along with the pre-established groups, of course, more spontaneous groupings can also be used.

Use Goal Cards Regularly. When students are working independently or in small groups, have them write their goals or steps they will follow for the activity on an index card that they keep face up on the desk. It's also useful to have them estimate the time it should take to complete each goal or step. Not only does that routine help students develop awareness of goal orientation and timing in their work, but it also provides a handy reference for teachers as they move around the room to monitor and assist students.

Teach for Smooth Transitions. Be sure you know how you would like the room to look as students leave to go to another class, go to lunch, or go home for the day. Teach students a process for putting materials away, straightening furniture, and sitting in place quietly until you verbally dismiss them. In a couple of minutes after students are ready for the transition, it's good to recap what they've learned, analyze their working processes, raise interesting questions that lead to tomorrow's lesson, give legitimate compliments, and so on. Results are well worth the few minutes it takes to ensure smooth transitions. Such routines result in a sense of order as well as an opportunity to solidify learning and to make important teacher-student connections.

Support Systems

Students learn—and grow—when they tackle work that is a bit beyond their capacity to complete independently. That is true for a very advanced learner and for a student who struggles mightily with academics. The job of the teacher, then, is two-fold. First, the teacher must continually ensure that work undertaken by an individual student is a bit beyond that student's reach. Second, the teacher must ensure the presence of support systems that guide the student to success. Once the student can succeed at a new level of proficiency, the process begins again.

Scenarios of Support Systems in the Classroom

There are an infinite number of supports that teachers use to bridge the gap between the learner and the unfamiliar. They exist to help students think more efficiently about their work, to teach, to model, and to encourage. Absent such support systems, students muddle in uncertainty. Clarity of understanding is hard to come by. Discouragement prevails.

Careful observation—kid watching—is important in providing appropriate scaffolding for students. There are many sorts of supports that stem directly from the teacher's planning and skill. Others,

while guided by teachers, come in the form of peer support. The goal of both is to provide assistance necessary for a student to grow in knowledge, understanding, skill, and the confidence necessary to sustain their growth.

Scenario 1. Ms. Haines is an inveterate student of her students. She uses checklists of skills and understandings to guide her observation of student growth and need (see Toolbox, Figure T.5). These checklists enable her to simultaneously keep track of where students are relative to important competencies and still to assign them work based on their readiness needs and interests. She takes notes on students as they work, using large mailing labels for the notes that she dates and identifies with student names. She files these in notebooks organized by student name. Over time, the chronological notes on each student become valuable tools for charting student need and growth patterns. She also makes it a point to observe students in nonclassroom settings. There, she sees facets of her learners that simply do not surface in the classroom. She occasionally asks students to write her a letter about their work and perceptions about class. She also sometimes asks students to have someone who knows them well fill out a questionnaire about them.

She observes with two key beliefs in mind: (1) her observations should focus on looking for student positives as much as on looking for student deficits, and (2) whatever she concludes from observations should be tentative because students will continually change and she should be looking for that change. From her observations, Ms. Haines develops teaching routines and support systems closely attuned to her students' varying needs.

Scenario 2. Mr. Shaughnessy consciously teaches for success. His goal is to provide a variety of supports that help students identify precisely what they need to do to continue striving for quality in their work. He uses checklists to help students focus on whether their work contains all required elements (see Toolbox, Figure T.6). He routinely uses rubrics to help students reflect on the quality of their work (see Toolbox, Figure T.7). When students have difficulty planning multistep tasks, he uses planning guides to help them sequence their planning more effectively (see Toolbox, Figures T.8 and T.9). Finally, Mr. Shaughnessy uses examples of prior student work, helping current students analyze both its structure and quality as a guide for their own thinking and planning.

Scenario 3. Ms. Rubin supports student growth in a variety of ways. She uses "word walls" that contain lists of key vocabulary in current topics of study. These enable students who are learning English, who struggle with spelling and writing, and who learn better with visual cues to find greater success in their work. She also has a "big idea" wall (see Toolbox, Figure T.10). Here, she and the students list key concepts in their units. They also propose possible generalizations or big ideas in what they are learning. One column contains proposed generalizations. Another has those generalizations and big ideas the students have come to accept as valid as they test ideas over time. In a third column are potential generalizations or big ideas students

have rejected. She posts concept maps, which she and the students sometimes develop together to help them see the flow of ideas in the unit (see Toolbox, Figure T.11).

Ms. Rubin also holds mini-workshops on topics and skills that some students need to complete work effectively. In some instances, mini-workshops review work already covered in class. In other instances, she uses them as a way to teach in an alternate mode for students who have not grasped an idea or skill. Sometimes the mini-workshops exist to push forward the knowledge, thinking, and skill of students advanced in a topic. Sometimes she asks particular students to come to a mini-workshop. Generally, she announces the topic of the workshop and invites anyone who feels it would be of benefit. Mini-workshops generally last no more than about 10 to 12 minutes.

Scenario 4. Mr. Eliason helps students learn to support one another in a variety of ways. In his class, one student serves as "Keeper of the Book" each week. That student is responsible for logging in homework assignments, key information covered in class, and questions and answers important to student success. Entries are dated and signed by the Keeper of the Book. When a student is absent or just needs a refresher about a class, the book is available for guidance. At various times, nearly every student benefits from entries in the class log, and so they take seriously their role in making the log work for others.

Mr. Eliason also helps students form study groups to support one another in understanding complex assignments and in reviewing for tests. He sometimes provides study guides for the groups. Sometimes he asks them to construct their own study guides, which he reviews to ensure appropriate focus. Sometimes he assesses study groups orally, calling on students randomly to see how various students are faring in the groups. Similarly, his students work in review and revision groups with teacher-provided peer critique guides (see Toolbox, Figure T.12) to review drafts of one another's products several days before they are due. This allows students to get and respond to focused feedback before turning in important work for a grade. Mr. Eliason sometimes varies questions on the critique guides to reflect varying needs and goals of students in the class.

Additional Supports for Learner Success

What follows are a few effective supports that ensure challenge and success for learners with varying needs.

Vary Materials. Over time, teachers can accumulate a variety of materials that support learning on a given topic. Media specialists can be very helpful in acquiring books and other materials on key topics at varied readability levels and in a range of interest areas. Tape recording key segments of text can help students who struggle with reading grasp essential ideas by listening. Similarly, using a highlighter to mark essential passages in text can help students frustrated with reading spend reading time wisely.

Use Graphic Organizers to Help Structure and Extend Thinking. When carefully developed to match learning goals, graphic organizers can be very helpful to students in understanding, organizing, and extending their thinking

about essential understandings in a topic. Organizers also can be excellent teaching tools to help students learn the tools of thought and communication necessary for school success (see Toolbox, Figure T.13).

Provide Survival Packets. Teacher-developed packets that distill key information, ideas, skills, vocabulary, and sequences in a unit can help some students master material more efficiently and with greater understanding.

Use Participation Prompts. It is helpful for some students to have question cues. That is, a teacher prompts a student's thinking by saying, "Jonah, in a minute, I'm going to ask you how you feel we should set up this problem. First, however, I want someone to tell me what sort of problem this is." By announcing the question in advance, the teacher gives a student time to gather thoughts. For students who are uneasy with responding, who are learning English, or who do better when they have time to organize their thoughts, cueing questions can be a lifesaver. Other participation prompts include Think Alouds (Pavelka, 1999), in which a teacher asks students to orally unpack their thinking as they problem solve, thus allowing students to see how peers are thinking about an idea or skill; and unison responses, in which a teacher asks the whole class to respond to a question in unison prior to asking for individual responses. Strategies like Think-Pair-Share, developed by Frank Lyman, also invite greater participation by more students. In this strategy, the teacher poses a meaningful question, asks students to write their ideas for a couple of minutes, follows by having two students compare their thinking, then reposes the question for discussion by the class as a whole. The strategy maximizes participation and also gives students an opportunity to extend their thinking by joining their ideas with those of their peers. (For more information, see http://curry.eduschool.virginia.edu/go/readquest/strategies/tps.html.)

Build Language Bridges. Make every effort to ensure that English language learners have a way to make sense of print and of oral information and instructions. "Bridging" the student's original language and English is critical. This can be accomplished by grouping the English language learner with at least one other student who speaks the student's first language as well as English, or even one who is learning English but is further advanced. Materials in the student's first language can be quite useful, as can translations or synopses developed by teachers of English as a second language or community volunteers.

Shared Responsibility in the Classroom

The teacher in a classroom is the professional. By definition and law, ultimate responsibility for what happens in the classroom rests with the teacher. Nonetheless, a wise teacher understands that virtually everything in the classroom will work better if it "belongs to us" rather than "belonging to me." Positive environment, clear communication, mutually agreed-on guidelines, clear routines, and plentiful support for success are huge factors in helping each student feel pride and ownership in the classroom. How-

ever, it is important for teachers to make clear that they are counting on each student to work with them as a team to improve the class every day. If 30 feel invested in what happens in a classroom, the odds are inestimably higher that outcomes will be better than if one feels invested and 29 wait for that one person to make things work. Early and often, the teacher who seeks to attend to affirmation, contribution, power, purpose, and challenge says to students, "Let's figure this out together. Let's make this *our* class."

Scenarios of Shared Responsibility in the Classroom

What follows are vignettes that illustrate ways in which teachers guide students in shared responsibility for classroom operation and mutual success.

Scenario 1. Mr. Bell reminds his students that things will go more efficiently in the classroom if everyone pitches in with daily chores. Classroom jobs rotate weekly among tables. Students at the table decide who will assume responsibility for each part of the job during the week. One table tends to plants and animals in the classroom. One distributes and collects materials. One is responsible for washing desktops and making sure furniture is straight at the end of the day. One records daily weather information from the class weather station. One sweeps the floor and generally straightens classroom materials as the day ends. One makes sure announcements are posted, messages home are handed out, and information that needs to go to the office is taken there. One attends to other requests by the teacher. The sharing creates a sense of team membership as well as class ownership and responsibility.

Scenario 2. Mr. Franken and his students hold class meetings to evaluate how the class is functioning and to solve problems. He can request a class meeting, as can students. They use the brief times to talk about how class routines are working, how they might adjust procedures to help everyone work successfully, and to solve problems that arise among students. Communicating with respect and positive intent are key rules for contributing in a class meeting.

Scenario 3. Ms. Rogerson talks with her students when she is going to be out of the classroom for a meeting or staff development session. She reminds them that she has two options when planning for a substitute. She can leave structured work that will be easy for the substitute to follow, or she can leave differentiated lesson plans, in which students will have to help make sure the classroom runs as it should. After all, the routines are familiar to the students, but not to the substitute. Students decide which option would be most productive for them in the teacher's absence. If they elect the more flexible schedule, they talk about roles each of them will have to play both generally and specifically to make the day productive. When she returns, she goes over notes from the substitute—notes that students know she will ask the substitute to leave—and everyone evaluates the quality of student leadership and responsibility in the results. She finds students take immense pride in their ability to guide the work of the group.

Additional Examples of Shared Responsibility

There are many ways to share responsibility with students in the classroom, including the examples that follow. Shared responsibility should include both environmental and academic issues.

Use Evaluation Checklists. Teacher- and student-developed checklists are useful in evaluating how particular procedures or segments of class time are working. Such formats can be used individually or as a focus of group discussion to review and assess procedures and the role of each person (including the teacher) in their success (see Toolbox, Figure T.14).

Involve Students in Scheduling Decisions. It can make a huge difference to the attitude of students if a teacher says something as simple as, "We will need to schedule a test on this unit no later than September 30, so I can spend time with the papers before report cards. Think about your schedules in the next couple of weeks, and let's set a date for the test that will work best for you." Similarly, a teacher might say to students, "I am not planning right now to provide class time for work on your projects. However, if you find as you work that you would like some time to discuss parts of the project with the class, or if you would like to schedule a peer-critique session on the projects, just give me a note with your specific request and I'll be sure to build time into the schedule to meet those needs."

Engage Students in Assessing Their Own Progress. Teachers can provide students with checklists of skills and help them develop increasing comfort in monitoring selected work for their own competencies in those areas. In addition, students and teachers can work together to develop guidelines and procedures for portfolios or exhibitions that enable students to demonstrate their growth over time. Such practices ultimately enable students to communicate with parents and teachers (e.g., in student-led parent conferences) about their development. In these ways, students can develop a clearer understanding of their own strengths and needs, a better sense of what they need to succeed in the classroom, and a stronger sense of the connection between their efforts and successes (Burke, 2000; Stiggins, 2001).

Help Students Learn to Set Their Own Academic Goals. Closely related to students' growing ability to assess their academic goals is their readiness to establish personal learning goals. In addition to building student self-awareness and control of their development over time, this ability enables students to modify class rubrics to include goals for personal growth and to participate meaningfully with teachers in individual goal-setting conferences at key times in the school year. Assessing progress and establishing related goals also can be a powerful shared tool for establishing behavioral and social growth and goals as well.

Looking Back and Ahead

Like the fox watching the Little Prince seeking to tame him, learners watch to see if we will try to build ties with them, if we are willing to invest in them, if we are able to affirm them. They want to know if we'll help them build a place where their contributions are significant, achieve a sense of power in a very large world, realize a purpose in their school lives, and stretch them so they move toward their dreams.

This chapter has dealt with the first step in meeting the child's request for personal investment. Classroom elements of environment, communication, guidelines, routines, support, and shared responsibility cannot be the end of the teacher's mission. Because we are teachers, we necessarily care about the ideas, information, and skills students need to master under our watch. Nonetheless, these classroom elements are so potent that their presence has the power to magnify our success in transmitting content, and their absence can negate even our best efforts at what we often think of as "teaching."

In subsequent chapters, we'll look at the role of curriculum and instruction in addressing the learner's need for affirmation, contribution, purpose, power, and challenge. We'll see how curriculum and instruction become a key "cog" in the teacher's endeavors to provide invitation, opportunity, investment, persistence, and reflection. It is the case, however, that *many* learners will respond to affective invitation and opportunity before they take the risk of accepting academic invitation and opportunity. For *most* learners, the pairing of affective and cognitive are inextricably bound. Great teachers seldom pretend to attend to one without equal attention to the other. Whatever disturbs that balance in our teaching disturbs our teaching.

5

Curriculum and Instruction as the Vehicle for Addressing Student Needs

As adults responsible for the growth of the next generation, we should know that we are not doing our jobs unless we provide youth with the opportunities to live right—that is, with chances to do their best. A just society is one in which men and women, rich and poor, the gifted and the handicapped, have an equal opportunity to use and to increase all their abilities, each according to her or his talents (Csikszentmihalyi, Rathunde, & Whalen, 1993, p. 260).

"Please tame me," says the fox.

If the world is right—if it is to *be* right for the child—the teacher agrees to form that bond with the student. The agreement is the first step. It is the teacher's contract with the child to care intelligently, unyieldingly, and deeply about the individual's strengths and weaknesses, dreams and nightmares, uniqueness and commonality. The teacher's agreement to make ties recognizes the learner's need for affirmation, contribution, power, purpose, and challenge. The agreement responds with a pledge to bring investment, invitation, opportunity, persistence, and reflection to the time, place, and interactions that will bind together teacher and learner. It sets the tone for what is possible. The agreement is the first step, a step of immense consequence, but it is a beginning.

Although the teacher's role bears some of the hallmarks of the counselor, parent, coach, social worker, and so on, those are not the teacher's central role. It is the mandate of the teacher to teach. Thus teachers shape lives, not by providing a sturdier network of social services, not by helping the child explore the psyche, not by standing on the sidelines and providing strategies designed to capture the game point, but by equipping students with the intellectual wherewithal necessary to make their way in a world that increasingly demands academic preparation for full societal participation.

As teachers, we teach. Our tools are not the analyst's couch and prescription pad, for example, but curriculum and instruction. We are charged by society to ensure that students develop the knowledge, understanding, and skill necessary to be fulfilled and productive members of society.

56

The charge is more circular than it seems on the surface, however. Only when we as teachers utilize the tools of our trade—curriculum and instruction—to ensure affirmation, contribution, power, purpose, and challenge, will we succeed in contributing significantly to the development of mind that is our charge. In other words, we rarely succeed in teaching subjects unless we teach human beings as well.

I had an algebra teacher in 8th grade who knew algebra well and was serious about her subject. Her class was a "tight ship." We were the embodiment of time on task. It is interesting that as I write, I cannot remember the teacher's name. I can, however, see her standing at the board. I can most assuredly feel the tightness in my stomach that was a part of every hour spent in her room. I did not feel affirmed in her class. I felt a growing incompetence that bore on me like a weight. I did not feel like a contributor. I had nothing of worth to share in that place. Had the teacher ever thought to have us work in small groups, I would have been always the student the others had to lug through the task. Never once did I see algebra making me a more powerful person. To the contrary, it stripped away what fragile confidence I might have carried into adolescence. It never occurred to me that the subject could be useful in the world beyond our class. I was not challenged; I was overcome. I studied hard, but that merely proved to me that effort made no difference and that I lacked the magical ability to connect with the escalating mysteries that came from the teacher's mouth and the

book, and that made their way to the blackboard.

That teacher knew her curriculum. She instructed with a bulldog-like intensity. She taught algebra. But she did not teach me. Hence, algebra became a part of my deconstruction more than it was instructive to me. Mrs. Wannamaker taught me German just a year later. *Her* name I remember well. I also remember the small and large attentions she paid to me. She always seemed sure I could be a successful language student and consistently gave me whatever work would prove that to be the case. She affirmed me with eye contact, smiles, and partnership in the daily tasks of the teacher—a dignity that suggested that my presence was somehow significant. As students in her class, we helped one another over weak points in our learning. We hosted a statewide language conference and found power not only in the immediacy of our task, but also in the myriad roles that drew on the best in each of us. We saw repeatedly how this new language connected with science and history and literature and music and the nightly news, with places we dreamed of traveling, with the vocabulary of our own language. The pace of the class and its variety were brisk, but challenge was an individual thing. This teacher constantly checked our understanding and proficiency and dealt with us as individuals to ensure that we had time, attention, and work that moved us along at what seemed to each of us a challenging clip.

These two teachers were solid with curriculum. They both instructed with confidence that signals kids "there will be no messing around in here." The difference was that the first teacher taught algebra. The second teacher taught *me* German.

I don't think it is a coincidence that I majored in German and have struggled with my attitude about math and my ability to do it since that algebra class. (I was, by the way, a competent and confident math student before that year, and I had been a relatively slack and uninspired Latin student before my encounter with German and Mrs. Wannamaker.)

"Please invest in me," I said to both teachers.

One teacher responded, "The information is here. I'll deliver it. You get it."

The other said, "I will learn about you and do whatever it takes, using this subject matter, to make sure you are a fuller and more potent human being than you were when you walked in this room. Please be my colleague in that quest."

There were at least five characteristics of curriculum and instruction in the classroom that genuinely helped me learn; the work was important, focused, engaging, demanding, and scaffolded. These characteristics were direct responses to my need for affirmation, contribution, power, purpose, and challenge. They were the concrete manifestation of the teacher's more abstract attitude of invitation, investment, persistence, opportunity, and reflection. Curriculum and instruction became the medium through which the teacher showed me the power of knowledge, the power of self, and the inextricable links between the two.

This chapter will examine these five characteristics of effective curriculum

and instruction. Again, feel free to modify the list of characteristics as you have come to see them (see Figure 5.1).

Curriculum That Is Important

We teach in our classrooms like hamsters in a wheel. There is more information in our disciplines to "cover" every year. We move as fast as we can, but we can never finish. The faster we move, it seems, the greater the expanse of information—the greater the expectation that we should be able to make the wheel turn faster yet. As Steven Levy (1996) reminds us, "We cannot teach the breadth of the entire world and at the same time achieve any depth of understanding" (p. 28). It seems to most of us that there should be so much more to learning than checking off a standard or making note that facts have been dispensed.

Rightly understood, the various disciplines we teach in school evolved for a purpose much richer than coverage. They help young and old alike answer the timeless questions of life: What is life about? Who am I in it? How do I matter? What does it mean to be human? How does the world work? How do I make a contribution to my world? (Nelson, 2001; Phenix, 1964).

The dash to the ever-receding finish line of coverage doesn't feel right to teachers. There is also ample evidence that scaling Everests of information is not effective for our students:

- The brain is inefficient at rote memorization and seeks instead to make meaning of information. If we don't

---
FIGURE 5.1

Curriculum and Instruction as the Vehicle

What Do the Elements Mean?

Important

- What we study is essential to the structure of the discipline.
- What we study provides a roadmap toward expertise in a discipline.
- What we study is essential to building student understanding.
- What we study balances knowledge, understanding, and skill.

Focused

- Whatever we do is unambiguously aligned with the articulated and essential learning goals.
- Whatever we do is designed to get us where we need to go.
- Both the teacher and students know why we're doing what we're doing.
- Both the teacher and students know how parts of their work contribute to a bigger picture of knowledge, understanding, and skill.

Engaging

- Students most often find meaning in their work.
- Students most often find the work intriguing.
- Students see themselves and their world in the work.
- Students see value to others in the work.
- Students find the work provokes their curiosity.
- Students often find themselves absorbed by the work.

Demanding

- The work is most often a bit beyond the reach of each learner.

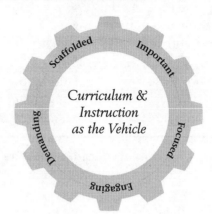

- Student growth is nonnegotiable.
- Standards for work and behavior are high.
- Students are guided in working and thinking like professionals.
- There is no "loose" time.

Scaffolded

- The teacher teaches for success.
- Criteria for success are clear to students.
- Criteria for classroom operation and student behavior are clear to students.
- Varied materials support growth of a range of learners.
- Varied modes of teaching support a variety of learners.
- Varied avenues to learning support a variety of learners.
- Small and large group instruction focuses on varied learner needs.
- Varied peer support mechanisms are consistently available.
- The teacher uses modeling, organizers, and other strategies to point out success.

---

make meaning of what we study, we are likely not to remember it, be able to retrieve it, or be able to use it (Given, 2002; Sousa, 2001; Wolfe, 2001).

- Students in schools, classrooms, and educational systems that teach less and teach it better score higher on standardized measures than students in schools that seek coverage of massive amounts of information with little emphasis on understanding. In other words, curriculum that is a mile wide but only an inch deep is ineffective in producing real learning (National Research Council, 1999; Stigler & Hiebert, 1999).

- As knowledge and information grow at an unprecedented rate, it becomes increasingly clear that "coverage" is an impossible educational goal. Rather, the aim of education must be to help students understand frames of meaning in the disciplines, how to ask useful questions, and how to find and use information effectively and efficiently (Erickson, 2002; National Research Council, 1999).

- To that end, it is the role of educators to "uncover" what is essential to know, understand, and be able to do in the disciplines. Experts of a field value such knowledge, understanding, and skill as essential to productivity in their discipline. Teachers must struggle against "coverage" and strive for "uncoverage" of meaning—distinguishing between what is essential to the discipline, what is important, and what would be nice to know if there were time to do so (Erickson, 2002; Tomlinson, et al., 2001; Wiggins & McTighe, 1998).

- The importance of curriculum lies in helping students master and retain essential information, organize knowledge around essential concepts, develop essential understandings, and competently utilize essential skills (Erickson, 2002; Tomlinson, et al., 2001; Wiggins & McTighe, 1998; Taba, 1962). Unless those elements are present, interrelated, and balanced in curriculum, students

weave a fabric of learning that is riddled with holes and is insubstantial.

- Important curriculum is necessarily focused on high-level thinking. There is no other way to ensure that students make meaning of, apply, and extend knowledge, understanding, and skill. In other words, there is no lesser route toward expertise in a discipline (Sousa, 2001; Tomlinson, et al., 2001; National Research Council, 1999).

Curriculum that is important, then, will help students come to know that

- What we study is essential to the structure of the discipline;
- What we study provides a roadmap toward expertise in a discipline;
- What we study is essential to building understanding in the discipline; and
- What we study balances knowledge, understanding, and skill.

Determining what is important in curriculum is the teacher's role. Difficult as it is, it is our responsibility (and opportunity) to probe the expertise of those whose work draws on and shapes a discipline to make clear to students the information, ideas, practices, products, and attitudes that are the signatures of that discipline.

Implicit in design of important curriculum for each student whom we teach is our belief that each of them is important—worthy of spending time doing what experts do. Thus begins the journey of ensuring that curriculum and instruction are vehicles to address learner needs for affirmation, contribution, power, purpose, and challenge.

Curriculum and Instruction That Are Focused

Once we know what is genuinely significant in a topic of study, our next job as teachers is to ensure that each step in the teaching and learning process is designed to guide students toward a high level of competence with the knowledge, understanding, and skill we have deemed critical. No more building sugar cube igloos if we and our students can't specify how that task results in essential knowledge, understanding, and skill needed for growing expertise in the discipline we are learning about. No more fascinating lectures that leave students wondering what they have just heard—and why.

In a focused curriculum, teachers specify precisely what students should know, understand, and be able to do as the result of a unit of study. This becomes the rudder to steer each segment of teaching and learning that follows.

Once a teacher is clear about what is essential to learn, he will pre-assess students to determine their group and individual strengths, weaknesses, understandings, and misconceptions (Stronge, 2002; National Research Council, 1999). Clarity about learning goals makes pre-assessment both easy and a nonnegotiable item in a strong classroom. How would we assume to teach individuals effectively with little sense about what they know, don't know, or misconceive related to what is essential in our study?

Armed with a better sense of where students stand relative to essential knowledge, understanding, and skill, a teacher can begin to craft lessons. Each lesson is, at its core, something we ask students to do, using a portion of key information, to come to understand an essential idea. And so we progress, step by step, lesson by lesson, to ensure that each student develops and extends the competencies specified as critical to the unit. At times, some students will pause in place to gain surer footing with an idea. The teacher may have all or some of the students practice a skill necessary to move ahead. She may reteach ideas for students moving less confidently through the sequences of learning, or extend the ideas for students advancing quickly. In any case, each step in the process is targeted to what is genuinely important to learn.

In the end, a teacher who crafts a focused curriculum asks students to produce something that demonstrates what they have come to know, understand, and be able to do as a result of the study. Once again, this product or demonstration calls on students to employ the knowledge, understanding, and skill at the core of the unit.

Whether one advocates developing focused curriculum with "backward design"—beginning with the final product or assessment and determining what is necessary for students to do to arrive there successfully (Wiggins and McTighe, 1998)—or one advocates specifying the essentials up front and moving ahead (Erickson, 2002; Tomlinson, et al., 2001), clarity of design is the goal. A focused curriculum causes students to understand that

- Whatever we do in this class is unambiguously aligned with stated, essential learning goals;

- Whatever we do in this class is designed to get us where we need to go;
- Both the teacher and the students know why we're doing what we're doing; and
- Both the teacher and the students know how the parts of the work contribute to a bigger picture of knowledge, understanding, and skill.

Implicit in focused curriculum and instruction is the message that the student's time is too valuable to waste and that the enterprise of helping each student become all she can become requires our best efforts at using all the learning opportunities available to us on what really counts.

Curriculum and Instruction That Are Engaging

Although gauging importance and establishing and maintaining focus have much to do with the integrity of curriculum and instruction, they have little to do with the magic of the classroom for kids. Learners are seldom lured away from play, video games, television, or daydreams by either the conceptual frameworks of disciplines or the promise of airtight focus on learning outcomes. Much of the fine art of teaching comes in figuring out how to deliver the curricular fundamentals in ways that are irresistible to young minds.

Phil Schlechty (1997) presents a formidable challenge:

> The business of schools is to design, create, and invent high-quality, intellectually demanding work for students . . . work that engages students, that is

so compelling that students persist when they experience difficulties, and that is so challenging that students have a sense of accomplishment, of satisfaction—indeed of delight—when they successfully accomplish the tasks assigned (pp. 49, 58).

Steven Levy (1996) talks about finding the genius of the topic and combining that with the genius of the teacher in an environment that is rich and varied enough to tap the genius of each student. In other words, he proposes that learner engagement occurs when a teacher sees what's really powerful in a topic, merges that with his or her own particular passions and talents, and creates a place of learning where there are enough materials, avenues, and inquiries to invite each student to use individual abilities and interests in mutual exploration of intriguing ideas.

However we conceive it, every lesson plan should be, at its heart, a motivational plan (Ginsberg & Wlodkowski, 2000). Young learners are motivated by a variety of conditions. Among those are

- Novelty (Sousa, 2001),
- Cultural significance (Ginsberg & Wlodkowski, 2000; Delpit, 1995),
- Personal interest (Sousa, 2001),
- Personal relevance or passion (Smith & Wilhelm, 2002; Clyde & Condon, 2000; Sizer & Sizer, 1999; Csikszentmihalyi, 1990),
- Emotional connection (Ginsberg & Wlodkowski, 2000; Given, 2002),
- Product focus (National Research Council, 1999; Katz & Chard, 1997; Schlechty, 1997),
- Potential to make a contribution or link with something greater than self (Ginsberg & Wlodkowski, 2000;

National Research Council, 1999; Levy, 1996), and

- Choice (Clyde & Condon, 2000).

Thus, when curriculum and instruction are engaging, students come to understand that

- I will most often find meaning in the work,
- I will most often find the work intriguing,
- I see myself and my world in the work,
- I see value to others in the work,
- I find that the work provokes my curiosity, and
- I find myself absorbed by the work.

When curriculum and instruction are important, focused, *and* engaging, teacher and students are poised on the brink of great possibility. Now the class is geared toward focused efforts on what matters most in the discipline—*and* what links the learner's world to the world of the expert.

Curriculum and Instruction That Are Demanding

Perhaps it is the stuff of being human, but we feel better about ourselves when we work hard. It makes us feel strong, worthy. Students not only have more respect for classes that are demanding, but they also have more respect for themselves when they are in those classes. Noted psychologist Mihaly Csikszentmihalyi reflects, "We believe each person knows quite clearly what it means to do one's best, and that everyone, given a chance, would like to savor that experience as often as possible" (Csikszentmihalyi, Rathunde & Whalen, 1993, p. 18).

There are at least two features to curriculum and instruction that are demanding. First, it is their design to teach each student what is worthy and essential in the subject. Demanding curriculum and instruction represent a plan to engage every learner in exploring, understanding, and mastering the facts, concepts, principles, and skills an expert in the discipline would value.

That means the teacher does not exclude any students from complex thinking. It is likely that we commit educational malpractice when we advocate, for example, that some students should consistently work at the lower levels of Bloom's Taxonomy (or any other one) and some should work at the higher levels. Only when we provide consistent opportunity for each student to sharpen his abilities as a thinker will each student develop into a fully thoughtful adult. For every student, that means persistent, meaningful, guided work that draws on the skills of complex thinking as well as the skills of thinking about thinking (Sousa, 2001).

Demanding curriculum and instruction also means the teacher ensures that every student develops the habits of mind and attitudes, or metaskills, necessary for success in school and in life. Those include such things as working hard, concentrating, being curious, persisting, working independently, enjoying work, being open minded, and looking at ideas and issues from various perspectives (Costa & Kallick, 2000; Csikszentmihalyi,

Rathunde & Whalen, 1993; Marzano, 1992).

In addition to ensuring that each student is focused on the framework of meaning and skill in a discipline, demanding curriculum and instruction also provide a plan for each student to experience success as a result of persistent hard work. There is no law or principle, of course, that says a student who slacks off from time to time is somehow diminished. And, of course, there is no guarantee—and no need—to be successful in all things all the time. Demanding curriculum and instruction, however, do intend to create for each learner a pervasive *pattern* of hard work (with engaging ideas, materials, and strategies) and a pervasive *pattern* of success.

In some perverse way, we educators often see teaching for success as a kind of "cheating," a watering down of otherwise substantial curriculum. To the contrary, it is imperative that we draw on what we know of human motivation.

When students believe they are capable of success with assigned tasks, they are more likely to persist. When they are convinced that effort will not result in success, they are more likely to give up on the task, thereby protecting themselves from humiliation. Further, they construct a belief that ability is a fixed trait, not mediated by effort. If they do not have the ability to do a task, there is nothing to be done about that, they conclude (Dweck, 1986). Said differently, when students become frustrated because a task is well beyond reach, they are likely to lose motivation and, in time, experience a decline in their level of

achievement as well (Csikszentmihalyi, Rathunde & Whalen, 1993).

Here, then, is the conundrum for teachers. How do we balance hard work and success? What appropriately demanding work for one student will be frustrating for another and will require no effort at all from a third?

Certainly a part of the answer is found when teachers build curriculum and instruction around essential frameworks of the discipline for all students and when teachers plan to scaffold success for all students from their point of entry. Although the goals of essential knowledge, understanding, and skill remain bedrocks for the class as a whole, the teacher makes adaptations in time, support, materials, and routes of access to ensure that each learner finds success at the end of hard work.

Curriculum and instruction techniques that are demanding include the following:

- Guide students in working and thinking like experts.
- Place the level of difficulty of work just beyond the reach of the learner.
- Make student growth nonnegotiable.
- Establish high standards for work and behavior.
- Eliminate "loose" time.

Curriculum and Instruction That Are Scaffolded

Great teachers consistently raise the ceiling of performance for each learner. At the same time, they raise the support system for each student. Placing work a bit out of the reach of a learner and then ensuring that the learner extends his reach and succeeds at the new level is at the heart of high-quality teaching.

Recently, a veteran teacher said to me that after teaching for over 20 years, the current school year was the first time her really advanced learners had ever needed her. In the quick pause before her explanation, I concluded that this particular group of bright kids was immature or perhaps "needy" of teacher attention. Her response sent my thoughts in a very different direction. "They need me for the first time," she explained, "because this is the first year I've ever given bright kids work that was challenging for *them*. Once I did that, I discovered that they need me just like all other students do!"

No student knows how to grow in a subject until a teacher makes necessary the growth and provides the support system that guides the growth. This teacher knew she had made an important discovery in her teaching that year. To the degree that she did her job for *every* student, *every* student would find her indispensable. She would, in other words, need to scaffold the growth of each child.

We scaffold growth when we follow a particular logic of thought. First, we know precisely where students need to arrive at the end of a lesson, a unit, or a year to continue developing expert-like knowledge, understanding, and skill in a discipline—and to achieve maximum personal growth in that area. Then, we determine where each student is at the moment in relation to the goals and in her personal development. Finally, we take action to ensure that each student

grows as vigorously as possible relative to both the learning goals and her personal development related to those goals. In other words, we ensure catalysts for growth—we scaffold it.

Teachers scaffold growth in a myriad of ways. We make sure students understand the learning goals and are aware of how each segment of their work contributes to their growth in achieving those goals. We use multiple modes of teaching and a wide range of teaching and learning strategies. We teach in small groups. We provide varied materials for students to gain access to ideas and information. We use varied groupings of students, depending on student need at a given time. We ask probing and clarifying questions. We help students develop effective study groups. We use vocabulary that helps learners develop awareness of *how* they are working and the ability to make adjustments in their work likely to support success. We talk about how to work and study effectively and efficiently when students have important tasks to accomplish. We describe what quality looks like, or guide students in doing so. We model processes and procedures. And often, we do several of these things at a time. We scaffold growth when we use our knowledge of where each student is relative to where he needs to be to support that growth. Because we teach many students simultaneously, we try—on our best days—to use varied forms of scaffolding to meet varied learner needs.

Curriculum and instruction techniques that are scaffolded include the following:

- Provide guidance for the teacher in teaching diverse learners successfully.
- Establish criteria for classroom operation that are clear to students and support their success.
- Include varied modes of teaching to reach varying learners.
- Utilize teacher modeling, organizers, and a variety of instructional strategies to reach varied learners.
- Use small group and whole group instruction as well as individual coaching to reach varied learners.
- Include varied materials to support growth of varying learners.
- Allow flexible use of time in response to students' varied rates of learning complex materials.
- Build in a range of peer support mechanisms to support varied learner needs.
- Provide varied avenues to learning and expressing learning to support differences among students.
- Specify criteria for quality work and coach students in achieving those criteria.
- Involve learners in establishing personal goals and criteria for their own work and assessing their progress according to those criteria.

Curriculum and instruction that are important, focused, engaging, demanding, *and* scaffolded give students lofty things to do, establish an environment crafted on relationships and procedures that maximize the likelihood of success, tap into what matters to the learner, and build bridges between today's realities and the vision of tomorrow's success. In such contexts, teachers "moderate the process, student by student," (Sizer &

Sizer, 1999, p. 109). In such contexts, students are inspired and encouraged to learn.

Curriculum and Instruction in the Face of Student Diversity

Two principles lie at the center of envisioning the role of curriculum and instruction in creating ties with students. The first is that the opportunity to be shaped by rich, defensible curriculum ought to belong to every learner. The second is that because learners, even of the same age, vary considerably, the opportunity to be shaped by rich, defensible curriculum will be diminished unless the learner interacts with it in ways that work for *that* learner.

In regard to the nature of good curriculum, the themes are remarkably similar in thoughtful books on how to teach English language learners, students from different cultures, advanced learners, students with learning disabilities, students from low-income homes, students who have given up on school, and students who constitute "the norm." Over and over again, the experts tell us: teach them to activate prior knowledge, to see their lives and experiences in the lives and experiences of others, to be inquirers, to make meaning of the subject, to build conceptual frameworks, to grapple with thought-provoking questions, to make sound judgments, to develop authentic products that have meaning to themselves and others, to be active learners, to work hard, and to strive for quality (Kottler & Kottler, 2002; Smith & Wilhelm, 2002; Tomlinson, et al., 2001;

Allington, 2001; Cole, 2001; Finnan & Swanson, 2000; Ginsberg & Wlodkowski, 2000; Beane, 1990; Hopfenberg & Levin, 1993).

Even this first principle is difficult to achieve. The second is vastly more difficult. Each of the experts reminds us in differing language that while we must teach the best we know to each child, we must also teach that child in the way that is best for him or her.

Care for the child, they tell us. But you can care only when you understand—what it is like to be a part of that child's culture, what it is like to be unable to speak the language of the classroom, what it is like to go "home" to a shelter every night, what it is like to wonder about things no one else in the classroom seems to ponder, what it is like to think steady thoughts only to have them sabotaged by print that scrambles on the page.

Make links with learners' interests, talents, and dreams, the experts counsel us. But you can only do that when you know what they care about, what they do that gives them joy, what they would wish for if they dared.

Provide the support system necessary to ensure systematic growth in knowledge, understanding, and skill, they say. But you can only do that if you take time to know what individuals know and don't know—can and cannot do—at a given time.

Expect great things of the learner. But you must know the precipice that separates boredom from challenge and challenge from alienation for an individual.

The simple truth is that we cannot affirm the learner, cannot afford the learner purpose, power, challenge, and contribution, unless we work to know the child. We cannot respond effectively to individual learners only with invitation, investment, persistence, opportunity, and reflection that are focused on the whole class. The potentially powerful vehicles of curriculum and instruction through which we connect with and guide young people are rendered largely impotent if we see them as one-size-fits-all solutions.

In the next chapter, we'll explore what it might look like when teachers begin with the premise that curriculum and instruction should be important and focused for all learners and then move to the corollary premise that it must be engaging, demanding, and scaffolded in ways that reach individuals.

6

Curriculum and Instruction as the Vehicle for Responding to Student Needs: Rationale to Practice

"All children can learn" does not mean "all children are the same." Furthermore, diversity is not merely about external characteristics. If we're really going to take this seriously, that means we start looking at diversity on the inside as well as diversity on the outside. Making this principle both a moral and intellectual part of the curriculum will require . . . a diversity of approaches, diversity of techniques, and diversity of teaching strategies (Reeves, 2002).

A fox-taming teacher—one who wants to create ties with students—certainly understands that individual learners bring individual needs, dreams, and potentials to the classroom. Further, such a teacher understands that classroom environment—including large and small acts of the teacher—will reach out to the individual learner or push the learner away. Such a teacher functions always with the student in mind.

That teacher also knows that preparation for a life of possibilities requires both affective and cognitive strength. In fact, creating ties in the classroom builds student confidence through both an escalating sense of personal worth (self-concept) and realization of personal power (self-efficacy). The teacher needs to understand that these two elements are intricately bound. How the teacher guides teaching and learning will inevitably sculpt the learner's sense of self-worth—and how the teacher directly and indirectly affects the student's sense of value will necessarily shape how the student learns.

Because you matter, the teacher says to the student, and because learning matters to you, I will do my best to

- Make sure I teach and you learn what is genuinely of value in a subject;
- Pique your curiosity about what we explore, capture your interest, and help you see daily that learning is inherently satisfying;
- Call on you consistently to help you become more than you thought you could become through dedicated work; and

68

- Be your partner, coach, mentor and taskmaster all along your learning journey in this class.

To do less than that, the teacher understands, is to send negative messages about who the child is and might become, the worth of that learner's time, and the importance of that child in the teacher's mission. To do less is to reject creating any ties—and to reject the student. To do less is to undermine engagement in learning. Conversely, to send messages recognizing the centrality of the individual in the success of the classroom and of the teacher is for the teacher to accept responsibility unequivocally for doing whatever it takes to build not only the learner's sense of worth, but also his or her sense of power as a learner.

This chapter explores some concrete ways in which teachers make certain curriculum and instruction are important, focused, engaging, demanding, and scaffolded to maximize the likelihood that each student is well served in the classroom—both as a human being and as a learner. It is important to note again that while the characteristics of effective curriculum and instruction are dealt with somewhat separately in this chapter, they are, in fact, tightly bound to one another and to learning environment and student affect. What makes learning engaging, for example, is likely to enhance its importance to the student, thus tapping motivation that, in turn, enhances the likelihood of success and a sense of affirmation.

A Scenario Where Work Is Important, Focused, and Engaging

Mr. Johnson and his 5th graders will soon study the topic of buoyancy in their science curriculum. The related text chapter contains a great deal of information, and it's often difficult for students to determine what matters most or how it all fits together. That problem is exacerbated by the fact that state standards emphasize somewhat different information than the book. Neither the book nor the standards provide mechanisms for ensuring students understand the topic as opposed to simply memorizing material.

To be sure that the work he and his students do on buoyancy is important and focused, Mr. Johnson specifies in his curriculum plans exactly what his students must know, understand, and be able to do related to the topic. He also frames some pivotal questions for his students to answer as the study progresses (see Figure 6.1). This process helps the teacher develop clarity about what is enduring and important in the topic versus what might be nice to know (Wiggins and McTighe, 1998). In turn, it makes it easier for him to help his students focus on what really matters.

Once Mr. Johnson is clear on what students must know, understand, and be able to do as a result of the unit on buoyancy, he is much better prepared not only to help students grasp what the unit is really about, but also to help varied students work in a variety of ways toward a common goal. For instance, now that

--- FIGURE 6.1 ---

Essentials for Mr. Johnson's Unit on Buoyancy

What Students Should Know

Vocabulary: sink, float, buoyancy, gravity, specific gravity, density, force, displacement, body, weight, surface area, system, hypothesis, variables

Facts and Information:
- When a body is placed in water, two forces act upon it.
- The force of gravity pulls downward on the body.
- The water that has been displaced by the body pushes upward.
- A small, heavy body will usually sink in the water, and a large, light body will usually float in the water.
- Although some materials like steel and concrete are heavy, ships made from these materials can float.

What Students Should Understand

- Two forces govern buoyancy: gravity and water displacement.
- Buoyancy is affected by changes in a body related to weight and surface area.
- Buoyancy is affected by changes in the water related to specific gravity.
- Buoyancy works like a system.
- When one element in the system changes, other elements will change.

What Students Should Be Able to Do

- Use inquiry and the process of science to solve problems related to buoyancy.
- Design and conduct a scientific investigation to solve problems related to buoyancy.
- Develop a hypothesis based on observation, experience, and understanding of events.
- Analyze and interpret results to draw conclusions.
- Write a scientific report based upon observation, experience, and understanding of events.
- Identify and use variables in experimental design to make sense of phenomena.
- Express key ideas about buoyancy in ways that demonstrate understanding.
- Use mathematical thinking in solving problems.

Essential Questions to Guide Exploration

- How do forces related to gravity and water displacement govern buoyancy?
- How do changes in surface area and weight affect buoyancy?
- How does changing the specific gravity of water affect buoyancy?

he knows the pivotal learning goals, he finds pre-assessment of student readiness a simple matter. Further, he has a roadmap for continually assessing student progress as the unit moves along. He may provide a list of key vocabulary, including brief definitions, for students who are learning to speak English or who have difficulty decoding text. For advanced learners, he will plan appropriate challenges that extend essential understanding rather than using extraneous activities to fill time. For students who struggle, he will plan multiple ways to teach and revisit the essentials. He will check each activity and product assignment against his list of nonnegotiables to guarantee a match between what he asks students to do and where students need to arrive by the end of their exploration of the topic. Although he may sometimes elect to have students discover a principle rather than presenting it to them at the outset of a lesson, clear articulation of the principles will nonetheless be critical as he brings closure to any lesson and as he helps students discover patterns in their learning. Time spent on determining the precise course of a unit may not feel "jazzy," but it inevitably establishes a framework for both student and teacher success (see Toolbox, Figure T.15).

Mr. Johnson also wants to enlist the curiosity of his students as the unit begins. "Open your books to page 115 and read Chapter 5" falls short of convincing many of his learners that this study will be worthy of their time and energy. Further, the students in his class vary widely in their experience, proficiency, and comfort with science. If he can make a link between science and their own lives, he believes, the students will be more invested in the unit—and more able to make analogies that support understanding.

Therefore, as the unit begins, Mr. Johnson asks his students to think of times when some event, circumstance, or change in their lives made them "sink"

or "float." He gives a couple of examples from his own experience to be sure the students understand the task. Students could draw and explain several such instances, write a brief story about them, present a soliloquy, or select another way of capturing what made them "sink" or "float" and get teacher approval of their plan.

As Mr. Johnson studies the student responses, he gains useful insights into some of his students' lives as well as information about ways in which various students opted to express themselves. He privately "invites" some students to be ready to share their examples, and then in class encourages others in the class to do the same. Ultimately, he guides the students in developing principles about what seems to make humans "sink" or "float." Then he tells the students they'd be figuring out principles about sinking and floating in science through the concept of buoyancy.

Additional Strategies for Important, Focused, Engaging Curriculum and Instruction

This scenario provides one image of a teacher who works to make curriculum and instruction important, focused, and engaging. A few more strategies that can be useful in achieving those goals follow.

Focus Student Products Around Significant Problems and Issues. A middle school math class studied a construction site near the school that seemed to be creating a potential for traffic accidents. While students participated in direct instruction on key computational skills as a whole and in small groups, they continued to study the site plan—examining numbers of vehicles in the area at various times of the day, traffic patterns, accident records, alternative approaches to the planned traffic flow, issues of cost, and so on. Ultimately, they made recommendations to the construction company and town council. Most of what they recommended was implemented.

A high school history class continually integrated interviews with their readings, lectures, and discussions. Students interviewed a wide range of people over time who had fought in various wars, lived through "turning points" in the history of the 20th century, experienced life under multiple forms of government, held leadership positions, represented widely differing views on important issues, and so on. The direct link between history and lives of real people made the issues and principles behind their study dynamic and important to the students.

Use Meaningful Audiences. Products crafted for an audience that is important to the student generally seem much more compelling and the work that goes into them much more important than when the teacher is the sole audience. Schools themselves are full of interesting audiences. A 1st or 2nd grader (or older student, for that matter) might practice reading a book aloud in order to read it to a kindergartner. A high school student might explain the basics of chemistry in a newsletter to be shared with middle school students whose science class introduces chemistry. An outstanding writer in the middle grades might submit her work to a high school writing group for feedback.

Beyond schools, there are many potential audiences in the community: clubs, special interest groups, senior citizens centers, galleries, museums, and so on. Parents and grandparents can become powerful audiences, especially when the teacher provides guidance on the types of feedback that would be helpful or of student learning goals for which they might look.

Help Students Discover How Ideas and Skills are Useful in the World. For many students, the words on the page of the textbook are flat and go no further than the margins. Skills are things in workbooks. When a Holocaust survivor talks with students about issues of human dignity, the words in the government text, history book, or novel suddenly take on a new dimension of importance. Experiencing the concept of "monopoly" by comparison shopping in catalogues or in a mall with a limited budget prescribed by the teacher makes the difficulties caused by monopolies much more relevant and bothersome. To hear a popular songwriter talk about connections between poetry and music makes poetry something to be pondered more than dreaded. Make certain also that the voices that speak to students of the utility of ideas and skills represent both genders and a full range of cultures—including the complete range of cultures represented in the classroom itself and beyond.

Provide Choices That Ensure Focus. There are many ways to give students choices of work while still ensuring that they work to master essential knowledge, understanding, and skill. Learning

Menus (see Toolbox, Figure T.16), Think-Tac-Toe options (see Toolbox, Figure T.17), and RAFTs (see Toolbox, Figure T.18) are three of many such vehicles. Constructed appropriately, students must focus on important knowledge, understanding, and skill, but may make choices about how they do so. Such choice is often highly motivating. It can also be helpful to both teacher and students to encourage students to contribute some of the options—again, so long as each option requires focus on specified learning goals.

Look for Fresh Ways to Present and Explore Ideas. Cartoons often drive home an important point in memorable ways. Use them to help students relate to key ideas in history, science, math, literature, vocabulary, the arts, and a range of other fields. Invite students to contribute to the collection. Ask students to role play, pantomime, or present interior monologues as figures from history and literature—or even as math signs and symbols, species from science, and so on. It works well for the teacher to use these approaches in presentation as well. Use children's books in all grades and subjects to make complex ideas approachable and to reveal stories of the people from many cultures behind important ideas, events, and innovations. Find photographs, artifacts, art, music, and poetry that represent key ideas. Use technology, varied media, and multisensory approaches to teaching and learning. Not only do such fresh and surprising approaches enliven a class, but they also inevitably spark students not reached by more traditional instructional avenues.

Share Your Experiences and Invite Students to Do the Same. As you teach about a topic, talk about books you love, places you've visited, people you admire, and ideas you think about that relate to the topic. If you've had difficulty with reading, studying, or staying motivated in the past, share with students what that was like and what you found helpful in "getting unstuck." Take time to be human with your students and give them time to do likewise.

A Scenario Where Work Is Demanding and Scaffolded

Mr. Johnson understands that he must begin planning his curriculum to ensure that work is important (represents the essence of the topic or discipline), focused (each segment of teaching and learning aimed squarely at student acquisition of essential knowledge, understanding and skill), and engaging (designed to enlist the interest of young learners individually and as a group). He also understands that even these good plans will fall short of maximizing the potential of each learner unless he also ensures that work for each learner is challenging and scaffolded. The trick in providing challenge, he knows, is to place tasks just a bit ahead of a learner's comfort zone. However, because the work is then a little too hard for the learner, he also must provide the support necessary to help the learner gain comfort and proficiency with tasks that at the outset seemed unachievable to him.

Several days into the study of buoyancy, Mr. Johnson gives all of his students hands-on tasks that call on them to explore and apply the relationship between density, water displacement, and buoyancy. Based on pre-assessment information, it is clear to Mr. Johnson that some of his students have a solid grasp of the key knowledge, ideas, and skills central to the unit. It is also clear that some students are still tentative in their understanding of the topic.

It seems unlikely to him that any single activity he develops would be appropriately challenging for all students. He wants all of his learners to do work that is focused on the essential underpinnings of the unit and that is intriguing to them, but he decides the specifics of the tasks would need to vary in order to make sure the work is "a little too hard" for each learner. At the same time, he wants to plan for student success. Thus, he would have to provide support systems to enable students to work through the difficulties and emerge with confidence in their products.

Mr. Johnson develops a two-tiered inquiry. The basic nature of the task is the same for both groups. He simply presents and scaffolds it in ways that would make demands on students and simultaneously support their success at their levels of entry into the task (see Figure 6.2).

Following the inquiry activity, Mr. Johnson plays the role of consultant for a company seeking to engage services for boat design and asks a wide range of students questions about his observations. In the end, he guides them to accurate statements about density, displacement, and buoyancy. Then he asks students to

work in triads of their own choice to recapture the "rules" about buoyancy for the class in several ways: restating the principle so it would be understandable to a younger audience, drawing a diagram to illustrate it, and making an analogy with rules and events in their own lives. He again monitors their work and selects one or two examples of each approach to share with the class and post on the walls for future reference as the unit progressed.

Mr. Johnson then provides additional challenge and support in three additional ways. First, students use a self-evaluation checklist to critique their own contributions to the design task (see Figure 6.3). The checklist was familiar to them from its use in past collaborative efforts. The teacher and his students modify the checklist through the year as they see the need to develop new collaborative skills. In addition, he often adds a particular criterion to checklists of individuals to reflect needs of specific learners. Individual students and working groups are invited to do likewise.

In addition, students use a familiar rubric to both guide and assess the quality of the work of their groups (see Figure 6.4). This rubric, too, evolves over the year to reflect particular unit goals and evolution of student skills. Mr. Johnson works with students individually, in small groups, and with the class as a whole to guide his students in planning the next steps in their growth.

Finally, Mr. Johnson provides several Web sites related to buoyancy at a computer "inquiry station" in the room. The sites are problem-oriented, and he labels them as appropriate for apprentices, journeymen, craftsmen, or masters. Students self-select sites based on their own sense of comfort with the topic, and their teacher encourages students to work among the sites to test and extend their understanding of the topic. Students could work alone or in pairs at the station during several appointed times of the day. In addition to providing a learning approach particularly appealing to some of his students, the station proves a safe way for students to try out and refine understandings and skills.

The expectation in Mr. Johnson's class is that all students will work hard and continually look for ways to

---

FIGURE 6.2

Mr. Johnson's Two-Tiered Inquiry on Buoyancy

The first version of the buoyancy inquiry below is more structured and guided than the second version. The second is also set up to be "fuzzier" in processes and goals. It also has some more complex requirements that extend the essential goals of the unit. Mr. Johnson serves as a consultant for Oceanic Transports, moving among all groups, coaching thinking, and taking notes for a concluding discussion in which he will comment on designs and ask questions of designers. Version numbers on the examples below did not appear on student materials.

Cover Letter for Version 1

To: Designers and Engineers of Floatin' Boats, Inc.
From: Oceanic Transports, Inc.
Subject: Design Contract

We are interested in securing the services of a design company that can help us carry cargo more efficiently. To be specific, we need boats that carry maximum weight. We understand that your company has expertise in boat designs of this type.

We will send a consultant from our firm to observe your work and bring back information to us for discussion in our board meeting. We look forward to working with you.

Sincerely,

Ima Wrecke
Department of Engineering and Design
e-mail: iwreck@aol.com

(continues)

FIGURE 6.2 CONTINUED

Version 1 Assignment

To win the design contract from Oceanic Transports, teams of two from Floatin' Boats need to design a boat to carry as many metal washers as possible. You will be given materials (aluminum foil, one piece per boat only) to make your boat. You will also have metal washers to represent cargo. Make one model. Test it. Figure out how to improve it. Use what you learn in your second model so that it carries more cargo than the first model. Keep trying to make better models as long as there is time. Below are guides to help you with your design work.

Make a guess (prediction) before you build your first design.

We think the most washers our first boat will hold is _____ .

Design your first boat and draw a picture of your design below.

Answer the following three questions before making your second model.

1. How many washers did Model No. 1 hold before sinking? _____

2. We think we can improve on our design by _____

_____ .

3. We think making these changes will cause the boat to carry more washers because

_____

_____

_____

_____ .

Now make your second boat and draw a picture of it below.

———— **FIGURE 6.2 CONTINUED** ————

Answer the following questions before making another model.

1. How many washers did Model No. 2 hold before sinking? _____

2. We think Model No. 2 did or did not (circle one) work better because _____
_____.

3. To improve this model, we think we should _____
_____.

4. We think this would make the boat better able to carry more weight because _____
_____
_____.

5. What is the largest number of washers one of your boats held? _____ How many
grams is that? _____

6. What is the least number of washers one of your boats held? _____ How many grams
is that? _____

7. What is the difference between the total number of grams in Questions 5 and 6? _____

8. What does this tell you about more efficient boat designs? _____
_____
_____.

If there's time, try your next design and test it.

What can we now tell Oceanic Transports about how we will design the most efficient
boat possible for them? _____
_____
_____.

This design experience has made us think of the following question _____
_____
_____?

(continues)

—————————— FIGURE 6.2 CONTINUED ——————————

Cover Letter and Version 2 Assignment

To: Designers and Engineers of Ideas that Float, Inc.
From: Oceanic Transports, Inc.
Subject: Design Contract

We are requesting that your firm, Ideas that Float, Inc., submit a design for construction of a ship's hull to Oceanic Transports. We are looking for an efficient ship design that can be used to carry exactly 10 large metal disks (the ship must sink when the 11th disk is added) that we ship for use in the power industry. Oceanic Transports will provide disks and materials for your use in constructing the hulls. It is suggested that materials estimates be based on models of 1"= 1' in order to estimate costs for the overall project. The construction contract will be awarded to the company that makes the most efficient (not elaborate) design. To complete your design work and proposal, you must submit the following:

1. A model of the most efficient hull based on your research.
2. A report that includes
   • Written directions, drawings, and notes for each model tested;
   • A calculation of the density of the metal used in hull construction;
   • A calculation in square feet of metal needed for the actual hull;
   • Cost estimates for the metal used to construct the ship (actual cost is $472.45 per square foot);
   • Estimated gross weight of the actual hull and flywheels; and
   • A calculation of the volume of water displaced by the full-size ship hull based upon measurement of the downward force of the scale model.

A consultant from our company will observe your design work, taking note of your ideas for discussion in our board meeting. We look forward to working with you.

Sincerely,

Ima Wrecke
Department of Engineering and Design
e-mail: iwreck@aol.com

Source: H. Andrew Johnson, Crozet Elementary School, Virginia. Used with permission.

grow—and that he is on a mission to help them do that. It is the quest for growth that matters most to him. He models that in his own life and in his work with students. That quest is evident in the tone of the class. Over time, his students, like the teacher, get more excited about good thinking and evidence of growth than about checking off easy right answers.

Additional Strategies for Demanding and Supported Curriculum and Instruction

This scenario continues the story of one teacher who works to make curriculum and instruction demanding and supported, as well as important, focused, and engaging. A few more strategies follow. They can help ensure that the work students do stretches them and that the

---
FIGURE 6.3

Student Self-Evaluation for Contributions to Group Work

Student:

Task:

Date:

	Excellent	Good	Not Helpful
I helped the group be clear about the task and its requirements.			
I helped the group develop a plan for working effectively.			
I used specific knowledge, understanding, and skill to contribute to the group's solution to the problem.			
I contributed directly to successful completion of the work.			
I listened carefully to the ideas and suggestions of others.			
I used time wisely during the work.			
I used resources appropriately during the work.			
I contributed to improving the quality of early ideas and plans.			
I helped solve problems the group had while we worked.			

stretching is supported such that it leads toward success.

Use Tiered Approaches. Tiering assumes that within a particular lesson or product, a wide range of students should work toward the same knowledge, understanding, and skills. However, it acknowledges the varied readiness levels of students in approaching the task and thus presents the work at different levels of difficulty. Thus, while essential outcomes are similar, the demands of the task are structured and scaffolded in response to learner need. Many instructional approaches can be tiered, for example: writing tasks, homework, learning

FIGURE 6.4

Science Inquiry Rubric

Level 1
<ul><li>Written explanations do not demonstrate basic knowledge or understanding of the topic.</li><li>Key vocabulary is not used or not used correctly.</li><li>Key skills are not used or are not used correctly.</li><li>Diagrams and notes are not included in the written work.</li><li>There is little or no evidence of attempts to raise questions in the notes.</li><li>There is little or no evidence of effective mathematical thinking in the work.</li><li>There is little or no evidence that the student carried out the activity.</li></ul>

Level 2
<ul><li>Written explanations indicate knowledge of facts at a basic level, but may show some difficulty in applying knowledge.</li><li>Key vocabulary is used and used correctly most of the time.</li><li>Key skills are used and used correctly most of the time.</li><li>Diagrams and notes are included, but may contain errors or show lack of organization.</li><li>Variables are not identified or considered in interpreting data.</li><li>Questions are raised, but there may be no plan for finding answers to them.</li><li>There is evidence of mathematical thinking that is correct most of the time.</li><li>The activity was carried out.</li></ul>

Level 3
<ul><li>Written explanations demonstrate a solid understanding of the topic, drawings and diagrams are labeled correctly, and significant questions for exploration are present.</li><li>There are clear indications that there is a rationale for the work, including observations, data, and consideration of variables.</li><li>There is substantial evidence that students have used inquiry and hypotheses in planning the activity and solving problems.</li><li>Connections are made to prior learning and this learning is used to help solve the current problem.</li><li>The task is successfully completed, including appropriate use of mathematics to collect and interpret data.</li></ul>

Level 4
<ul><li>Written explanations clearly indicate solid knowledge, understanding, and skill related to the topic, with accurate drawings and diagrams used to effectively communicate data, observations, and conclusions.</li><li>Knowledge, understandings, and skills are applied appropriately to solving problems in unique and effective ways.</li><li>Connections are made to prior learning, which is applied appropriately to solve problems.</li><li>Investigations are guided by a quest to answer important questions, and notes provide evidence that questions are linked to show relationships between observable variables that can be tested through stated hypotheses and that lead to additional investigations.</li><li>Mathematics is used as an effective tool in the scientific process.</li><li>The task is completed at a high level of effectiveness, efficiency, and thought (elegance of solution).</li></ul>

centers, computer tasks, product assignments, learning contracts, and labs, to name a few (see Toolbox, Figure T.19).

Incorporate Complex Instruction. This strategy begins with rich, high level, multifaceted tasks and supports learner success in meeting requirements by linking tasks directly with individual strengths, providing peer support, and teaching competencies necessary for increasingly independent work (see Toolbox, Figure T.20).

Use a Variety of Rubrics to Guide Quality. There are many kinds of rubrics, among them, task-specific rubrics and more generic ones. Task-specific rubrics help students focus on quality in particular endeavors. Generic rubrics, as well as the task-specific rubrics, provide students with elements of successful work and descriptors of how those elements might look as they escalate from minimally acceptable to expert-like. Generic rubrics, however, are designed to be used throughout a year (or longer) and often across multiple subject areas. Continual use of such rubrics allows teachers time to teach about the various elements and how students can continue personal development in them, and to modify the rubrics as students develop in proficiencies over time. Likewise, they allow students ongoing opportunity to become comfortable with a language of scholarship and productivity and to see how their work can grow in those important areas (see Toolbox, Figure T.21).

Provide Learning Contracts at Appropriate Times. Learning contracts allow teachers to focus students on work necessary for their own development and growth at a particular time. Generally all students work on contracts at the same time, but tasks on a given student's contract will be focused on that particular student's needs. Some tasks may be on everyone's contract. Other tasks may be particular to a small group of students in the class (see Toolbox, Figure T.22).

Aim High. It is likely that we underestimate what any student can accomplish, often establishing as performance ceilings goals that ought to be planks in the floor. That is the case for advanced learners, students with learning problems, English language learners—and teachers, for that matter. It is highly likely that students achieve much more when we present them with tasks that we genuinely believe to be beyond them, and then set out to ensure their success on those tasks. Aiming high means, at least, that all tasks require serious thought, that they deal with important ideas, and that they cast students as problem solvers. For advanced learners, it means teachers need to develop tasks at a level of abstractness, complexity, fuzziness, and more, which may seem to the teacher out of her own reach.

Take a "No Excuses" Stance. Accepting no excuses for work that is undone, incomplete, or inferior is trickier than it might seem. Seen correctly, "no excuses" is not punitive, but redemptive. There are students whose handicaps make some tasks daunting, if not impossible. There are too many students whose home circumstances are unthinkable and impose great stress in their lives.

Some bright learners balk at genuinely challenging tasks because they have not had to struggle with schoolwork before, and they lack both the tolerance and skills for serious striving. In these and other instances when students provide excuses for inadequate work, the teacher is not without compassion for circumstances, but conveys, "I understand. I wish it weren't difficult. But I also know that you will be a stronger person for working through the difficulties rather than allowing them to make you less than you could be." A no-excuses teacher is formed with one part Mother Superior and one part Marine Drill Sergeant at the core. The message is not so much, "If you don't do the homework, I'll line up zeroes in the grade book," but rather, "If I need to provide a time, place, and support system in this room to make sure the homework or the project gets done, so be it—but the work *will* get done." A great classroom conveys to all students, "This is hard, but you can do hard things, and I am not willing to let you settle for less." Enabling students to succumb to excuses empowers the problem that already diminishes their vision of a possible future.

Become Computer Savvy. Computers offer so many ways to ensure that work is both demanding and scaffolded. Seldom do all students use a computer or program in the same way at the same time. Webquests offer amazing opportunities to tap into student interests, extend understanding and skill on a broad range of topics, and present work at differing levels of demand, while focusing all students on meaningful and interesting tasks. (Webquests were originated by Bernie Dodge at San Diego State University. To learn more about them, go to http://webquest.sdsu.edu.)

For students who are more advanced as independent learners, Web Inquiries encourage students to play a more seminal role in shaping their own inquiries. Developed by Philip Molebash of San Diego State University, the Web Inquiry format coaches teachers in guided or open inquiry. For more information, see http://edweb.sdsu.edu/wip/.

Appropriately monitored, the Internet provides endless resources that can link with students' interests, experiences, and primary languages. Further, there are high-quality programs (and certainly some of lesser quality) that enable students to build knowledge and skills in an array of subjects, as long as the teacher assesses students' needs and matches task and program to those varying needs. Some programs also provide voiced text. Computers also add additional ways a teacher can present ideas to students in front of the whole class and in small group settings.

Help Students Realize Success Is the Result of Effort. The most successful students understand that their success results from their own effort. Although they will not succeed 100 percent of the time, they know that their continued effort is likely to lead to success. Students who have been less successful in school often attribute success and failure to luck, teacher bias, chance, and lack of ability. It's critical to student success that each student realizes his or her persistent effort is linked to success. That means teachers must routinely help students who struggle academically to develop goals just beyond their reach, support them in achieving those goals, and then celebrate their accomplishment. Likewise, it means that teachers must guide advanced learners in doing the same. This principle challenges how teachers think about school, perhaps like no other in differentiation, but it is absolutely central to classrooms in which teachers are determined to help young people become all they can be.

Use the New American Lecture Format. When lecture is the most appropriate instructional strategy, be sure (1) that the lecture is well organized to clearly present key knowledge, understanding, and skill; (2) to provide students with a blank graphic organizer that follows the flow of the lecture; (3) to guide students in completion of the organizer as the lecture progresses; and (4) to stop often during the lecture to ask students to review ideas, make predictions about what will come next, and make links with past knowledge or their lives. Such an approach uses the lecture as a tool that teaches about learning as well as one that maximizes learning. (For more information on the New American Lecture, see Silver, et al., 1996.)

Designate a "Keeper of the Book." Each class period, designate a student to be "Keeper of the Book." As discussed in Chapter 4, this student will record the date, a list of homework or other assignments, and the important knowledge, understandings, and skills explored in class during that period. This provides a wonderful support system for students who are absent and for students whose readiness to follow the progression of a class is fragile for any reason. The book is kept where students can get access to it as they need it. The process also involves students in an important role in the smooth operation of the class, as they provide a service to peers. It helps them listen for important ideas, and it is a great help to the teacher in dealing with absentees and a range of students who need support in grasping the flow of a class.

Try ThinkDots. ThinkDots is one of a number of instructional strategies that can be of high interest to students as they work toward competence in knowledge, ideas, and skills. The ThinkDots strategy provides peer support for students as they work collaboratively on a task and also asks students to work in a fresh way as they learn (see Toolbox, Figure T.23).

Directly Teach Strategies for Working Successfully with Text. Many elementary and secondary students are stymied in their academic work because they are ineffective with reading text materials. Any teacher who wants to ensure learner success simply must learn to teach the skills required for competence with texts to any student lacking those skills. There are many factors in helping students learn to navigate text materials, including:

- Surveying a chapter (or other segment) to determine its structure (for example, using titles, subtitles, pictures, and other graphics to make meaning);

- Predicting what will be in a chapter (or other segment) based on the survey;
- Asking questions as they read, based on their thinking and the structure of the chapter;
- Locating hard and important words;
- Finding main ideas;
- Finding details that flesh out main ideas;
- Linking ideas in the text to personal experience and prior knowledge;
- Summarizing important ideas;
- Determining the structure of meaning or flow of ideas in the text material;
- Monitoring one's attention, thinking, and understanding while reading; and
- Making adjustments in reading in response to self-monitoring.

There are many ways teachers can focus student attention on these critical skills. One is use of multiple-entry journals through which students are guided in reading and writing with particular skills important to their development as fluent readers of text (see Toolbox, Figure T.24).

Use Think Alouds. This strategy asks students to verbalize their thinking as they encounter and grapple with problems. The problems may be mathematical, but also may involve making meaning of unfamiliar or complex text, deciding how to organize ideas for a presentation, determining how to study for a test, or seeking to make a wise decision. In a Think Aloud, the speaker assesses what is familiar in a situation ("What do I see here that's helpful?") and what is uncertain ("What doesn't seem clear to me?"), draws on current knowledge and

skill ("What resources or approaches can I use to help me here?"), predicts ("What seems likely to happen next?"), and so on. It is often helpful for teachers to model Think Alouds in varied contexts throughout the year—not only demonstrating the strategy, but also sharing proficient avenues of thought. As students begin to present the Think Alouds themselves, they may "unpack their thinking" just for themselves (on tape or in writing), use student-to-student Think Alouds in pairs or small groups, take part in student-to-teacher Think Alouds as teacher and student assessment device, join a teacher in presenting a Think Aloud for the class or small group, or contribute to whole class understanding. (For more information on Think Alouds, see Burke, 2000; Pavelka, 1999; or http://www.lessonplanspage.com/ MathNumReasoningProbSolvingThink Alouds69.htm.)

Use Small Group Instruction as a Regular Part of Instructional Cycles. Because students vary greatly in readiness at any given point in an instructional cycle, it is critical during a unit to find a way to teach to a learner's need rather than only to an imaginary whole-class readiness. The principle of flexible grouping (that is, students consistently working in a variety of groups based on readiness, interest, and learning profile, and both homogeneous and heterogeneous in regard to those three elements) is central to the concept of defensible differentiation. It is important to students to see themselves in a variety of contexts, and important to the teacher to observe a student at work in different settings. One part of flexible grouping in most classrooms should be the use of similar readiness instructional groups that change frequently as the focus of instruction changes. Although this is only one facet of flexible grouping, it is important to ensure appropriate challenge and support on an ongoing basis for each learner (for example, see Schumm, Moody, & Vaughn, 2000). Using readiness-based instructional groups is also very beneficial to students with learning disabilities, students learning English for the first time, advanced learners, and a wide spectrum of other students. It is also critical that teachers of older students use small group instruction to help teach the fundamental skills of literacy and numeracy if those students have not learned them appropriately in earlier grades.

Mini-lessons or mini-workshops on particular skills are also a useful tool. In these instances, a teacher quickly convenes an instructional group based on observation of need. For example, a teacher might note that some students are having difficulty using the index of a book, or are stuck as they try to determine a focus for a project or paper, or have gotten rusty with multiplying fractions. In such instances, the teacher simply says something like, "I think I can help some of you who are a little bogged down with your topic. Come join me in the front of the room if you think it would be useful to brainstorm for possible topics for your project." The session might last only 10 minutes, and that particular instructional group would likely not meet together again, but a specific need has been addressed in a short time span, and students can move along more competently with their work.

Establish Peer Networks for Learning. Helping older students form study groups and providing structure and guidance for effective group study can greatly assist students who tend to feel alone academically and who bog down as they study because they have no network of academic peers to whom they can turn for clarification. With students of a range of ages, reading partners can be useful. Students may take turns reading portions of text and questioning one another about what they have read. They may engage in unison reading of a passage—or "echo reading," in which one student reads a line and another echoes or repeats the line.

Think-Pair-Share strategies also promote shared learning. In this strategy, a teacher poses an open-ended question essential to the topic at hand and asks students to think about the questions and jot down their ideas about it for a minute or two. Next, the teacher asks students to pair with a partner (who can be random or designated) and tell each other their thoughts. Finally, the teacher calls the class back together and asks the question again, inviting anyone to share ideas. Such strategies involve many more students in thoughtful class participation and in learning from one another.

Promote Language Proficiency. There are many ways to support language development. Among them are the following:

- For students learning a language, have items in a classroom labeled (with the appropriate article—a, an—as a part of the label) and post schedules, routines, and other guides to which students might often refer.

- Use key vocabulary lists and concise definitions for units of study to help students develop both language proficiency and focus on what matters most in a unit.
- Post ideas written in complete sentences and complex questions to model both for learners.
- Use highlighted texts in which the teacher has marked with a highlighter critical passages, enabling students with developing English (as well as other students with reading problems, learning disabilities, attention disorder, and so on) to focus on critical information rather than sinking in despair at the prospect of reading 20 to 30 pages of unintelligible type.
- Encourage students to express ideas on paper fluently and freely before reviewing form and structure. This can be more encouraging than cutting off ideas by premature attention to mechanics.
- Have students tell stories or summarize ideas while the teacher writes what the student speaks. The student then uses the manuscript to practice reading, develop vocabulary, and review ideas.
- Use visual cues such as icons, pictures, and organizers as you present or explain information. Label the visuals with key vocabulary or phrases. (For additional ideas, see: Bell, 2002–2003; Schoen & Schoen, 2002; Cole, 2001.)

Use Weekend Study Buddies. Teachers can develop canvas bags or shopping bags with materials designed to assist a student with particular learning needs.

The students then take the bags home over the weekend. When feasible, the bag may contain directions for parents to help their children with the materials. Contents of study bags might include familiar books for students to reread, flash cards for math, an audiotape of an explanation or story, a request for a letter the student might write to the teacher on a designated topic, and more. For advanced learners, the bags might include interesting readings on a topic about which the student knows a great deal, Web sites for additional research, complex questions to which the student might pursue answers, unique applications of ideas or skills, and other ways to extend learning and stretch the learner's perspective. For any student, a bag might include high-interest tasks. Only a few students on a given weekend would receive a study buddy. Presented appropriately, the study buddy sends a message that the teacher is thinking about and cares about the learner. For older students, portfolios can be used to develop and provide Study Extensions. (For additional information, see Stephens & Jairrels, 2002.)

Make Peer-Critique or Peer-Review Sessions a Regular Feature. It's worthwhile to ask students to bring a draft project to class a few days before the final version is due so that one or more peers can review the work to ensure that all necessary parts are present and that work is of high quality. Provide a peer-critique form to guide the review of the work based on previously designated elements and criteria (see Toolbox, Figure T.14).

Cue and Coach Student Responses. Students are both stretched and supported if teachers ask questions of varying complexity in class discussions. In addition, students find themselves challenged if teachers coach for expanded answers rather than accepting the first response of a learner. For example, saying, "Tell me more"; "Please explain your thinking there"; "What evidence can you show us for your answer from the text or our discussions"; or "How do you know this to be true" causes students to dig into their thinking rather than participate on a surface level. When a student is reluctant to speak in class, cue the student's response by indicating that a question is coming up. In some cases, the cue might even be to let a student know one day that you're going to call on them for a specified question the next day. Allowing students who need time to prepare the opportunity to succeed is, of course, important to their willingness to participate in the future, to their image with peers, and to their own sense of self as a learner.

Team with Resource Specialists. It's interesting how many solid instructional strategies benefit multiple learner needs. For example, some vocabulary development approaches may help students who are deaf, who have learning disabilities, who have difficulty attending to tasks, and who are learning English. Nonetheless, the classroom teacher cannot be expected to know the broad repertoires of strategies (or the knowledge and research behind them) that are the daily fare of special educators, educators of the gifted, reading specialists, teachers of English as a second language, and so on. Invite specialists to come into your room, get to know your learners, teach with you, and share strategies that can help students with whom they specialize—as well as others.

Looking Back and Ahead

"Please invest in me," says the student.

Once they agree, teachers are guided by three assumptions:

1. Because I see your value, I will connect with you.
2. Because I see your uniqueness, I will come to you on your own terms and in accordance with your own needs.
3. Because teaching is part of connecting, I will honor you by teaching you what matters most in your life.

In essence, these are the three "cogs" or "gears" that drive the concept of differentiation. They are inseparable. Rarely would a teacher's action serve one well without serving all three well.

In the final chapter of the book, we'll take a look at the "big picture" of differentiation. We'll look, too, at how the gears work in concert with one another.

7

The Simple, Hard Truth About Teaching

(The teacher) is able to take each student on his or her own merits, to convey, not a generic hope, not a one-size-fits-all confidence, but the specific version which can only come from the student's own facts and from knowing each child well (Sizer & Sizer, 1999, p. 114).

The conversation between the fox and the Little Prince is so simple, so basic. Yet it is the root system of responsive or "differentiated" teaching, because it is the core of high-quality teaching—and high-quality teaching and responsive teaching are really one and the same. It rests on this. What is essential in learners is difficult for teachers to see. Teachers accept responsibility for students about whom they genuinely care.

Those of us lucky enough to make connections with students once or twice or three times know this to be true, because its truth shaped our lives forever. Those of us who live our professional lives in classrooms know this to be true because of our observation of classrooms that captivate and extend the capacities of each student in them. We know it to be true from research.

In his book that encapsulates research on effective teachers, James Stronge (2002) defines effectiveness as creating a positive effect on student achievement as well as other important outcomes that have positive and lasting effects on the lives of students. Stronge says that research tells us the following:

- Students consistently want teachers who respect them, listen to them, show empathy toward them, help them work out their problems, and become human by sharing their own lives and ideas with their students.
- Caring teachers who create relationships with their students enhance student learning.
- Effective teachers consistently emphasize that their love for their students is a key element in their success.
- Teachers who create a warm and supportive classroom environment tend to be more effective with all students.
- Caring teachers intentionally develop awareness of their students' cultures outside of school.

- Effective teachers spend a great deal of time working and interacting directly with students.
- High levels of teacher motivation relate to high levels of student achievement.
- Teachers' enthusiasm for learning and for their subject matter is an important factor in student motivation that, in turn, is closely linked with student achievement.
- Teachers whose students have high achievement rates consistently talk about the importance of reflection on their teaching.
- Effective teachers have a solid belief in their own efficacy and in holding high standards for students. This is common among reflective teachers.
- Effective teachers carefully establish classroom routines that enable them and their students to work flexibly and efficiently.
- Effective classroom managers increase student engagement and maximize use of each instructional moment.
- Effective teachers clearly identify learning goals and link them with activities designed to ensure student mastery of the goals.
- Effective teachers use a variety of support systems to ensure student success.
- Effective teachers emphasize hands-on learning, conceptual understanding, and links with the world beyond the classroom.
- Effective teachers develop and call on a wide variety of instructional strategies proven successful with students of varying abilities, backgrounds, and interests.

- Effective teachers set high expectations for themselves and their students with an orientation toward growth and improvement evident in the classroom.
- Effective teachers are more concerned with student understanding of meaning than memorization of facts.
- Students achieve at higher rates when instruction focuses on meaningful conceptualization and builds on their knowledge of the world.
- Student engagement is higher when they take part in authentic activities linked to the content under study.
- Teachers in schools with high achievement rates pre-assess in order to do targeted teaching.
- Effective teachers know and understand their students in terms of abilities, achievement, learning preferences, and needs.
- Effective teachers reteach material to students who need additional help.
- Effective teachers use a variety of flexible grouping strategies to support student learning.
- Effective teachers demonstrate effectiveness with the full range of students in their classes.
- Effective teachers match instruction to learners' achievement needs.
- Effective teachers accept responsibility for student outcomes.

Charlotte Danielson, in her framework for enhancing student achievement (2002), describes "exemplary" instruction this way:

> All students are highly engaged in learning, and make material contributions to the success of the class by asking questions and participating in

discussions, getting actively involved in learning activities, and using feedback in their learning. The teacher ensures the success of every student by creating a high-level learning environment; providing timely, high-quality feedback; and continuously searching for approaches that meet student needs (p. 113).

It's really all quite simple. Learning is hard work. People learn better when they feel valued and supported. To value and support learners, we must know them. We honor learners by caring for them as they are and simultaneously expecting more of them. People learn differently. Teaching is more efficient and effective when it matches learner need. To teach academically diverse learners well, teachers must teach flexibly. Virtually all learners benefit when they learn in places with high instructional ceilings and lots of ways to climb to the top.

It's really quite simple. Teaching is about building sound lives through the medium of the most worthwhile knowledge, understanding, and skill. That happens learner by learner as we show each learner how learning has meaning in his or her life and how that life takes on new meaning as it grows in the power of learning. Or it doesn't happen for too many learners.

It's really quite simple. Effective teaching is responsive teaching. It begins with creating ties to each child. It begins with taming the fox.

Then Why Is It So Hard?

In truth, of course, living the simplest truths is seldom easy. That is certainly the case in the classroom. Most of us who teach believe that caring is integral to nurturing the young and to learner success. We *mean* to care. But it's hard to care deeply about the kid whose questions make us feel dumb. It's hard to care deeply about the child whose temper destroys the tone of the classroom in an instant. It's difficult to care about the child whose demeanor seems threatening, the one who stares with blank eyes, and the one who literally says, "I hate you." It's hard to care because we don't know how to see through someone else's eyes, to speak someone else's language, to make the world better for a child whose world is out of control. It's hard because there are too many students to connect with. It's hard because there is barely time to survive between the race that begins with the first bell and ends so long after the last bell rings. It's hard because people at home need so much of us too, and there seems never to be enough of us to go around, even for those people who are at ground zero in our lives, let alone those who inhabit the perimeters of our lives.

It's hard to form ties with students, teach responsively, and become exemplary, because we were seldom, if ever, taught that way ourselves. We have no images of how it should look. Further, we were not *taught* to teach that way, and, in fact, were often discouraged from developing the very habits of flexibility we needed to develop in order to become the teachers we dream of being.

It's hard because we are beset with political and societal messages that seem to counter all we know about good teaching, elegant instruction, the centrality of the human in the classroom. It's hard to do what conscience dictates when we fear we—and perhaps our students—would be punished if we did.

And, of course, it's hard to teach well, because teaching well is living well, in a classroom, surrounded at a given time by 30 young people who study our every move with far greater intensity than they ever muster for our lessons about math or history or art. Simultaneously, we seek insight about and passion for subjects we studied but never knew as practitioners, look for wisdom to shape the lives of young people who are not our own and who will be moved away from us at about the point we can pretend—in the best of circumstances—to know them, and through trial and error seek to develop the managerial skills beyond those necessary to run a large corporation.

So of course it's hard to teach. It's likely impossible always to teach well, to teach responsively, to differentiate instruction to the benefit of each learner in our charge. To make matters worse, there is no formula for excellent teaching—for responsive teaching. We cannot buy the book or take the course that shows us the answers. There are ideas, of course, for how we might go about responding to the myriad needs of learners in today's classrooms (so many, in fact, that the volume itself is discouraging). There are principles that will likely serve us well in our quest to become responsive teachers. But there is no textbook or lesson plan that can do the work for us. There is no magic set of instructional strategies that will solve our problems. There is no behavior management program that can begin to substitute for building relation-

ships of trust and respect with individual human beings. We simply have to decide the shape we want our teaching careers to take, and begin moving in that direction.

And here is our guarantee. The more promising for students our decision is, the more complex it will be to live out. The more fully professional we want to become, the greater the risks we take. The more artful we want our work to be, the clumsier we will look along the way.

But there is one more guarantee. The more willing we are to take the risks, the better the lives of our students are likely to become, and the greater the fulfillment we are likely to feel at the end of the day.

A Final Metaphor or Two

One of the things I like best about the encounter between the fox and the Little Prince is the ambiguity at times about who is the teacher and who is the learner. It helps me recall that as teachers, we are never fully "in charge" of what happens in the classroom. Our best lesson plans evaporate in the face of a riveting question from a child whose age is not a quarter of our own. Our persistence is reshaped by the persistence of a child who struggles mightily to walk across a room or speak in fluid sentences. Our humor is honed by the child who most tests it. In other words, each day, *we* are refashioned in our own classrooms.

If we allow ourselves to fall in love with what we do, we will be reborn countless times, almost always in a form stronger and more fully human than the one that preceded it. Thus it may be that to teach more responsively, more effectively, we ultimately need to accept two challenges. First, we need to cultivate passion for what we do. Second, we need to remove our protective armor and allow our students to shape us, reflecting on and learning from what we see.

Ray McNulty, former commissioner of education in Vermont and still a teacher at heart, tells a wonderful story about his mother. It is a marvelous metaphor for what happens when we cultivate passion for what we do.

McNulty grew up in an ethnic neighborhood in Boston. His mom was Italian, and he always knew—just as the other kids in the neighborhood knew—that his mom made the best spaghetti sauce in the neighborhood known for its fine sauces. In his neighborhood, spaghetti sauce is called "gravy."

When McNulty's mom made gravy, everyone wanted to come over for dinner. When he left home for college, he learned quickly that he had left a culinary treasure behind. His mom made sauce for him, packed it in dry ice, and mailed it to her son. He was so grateful for the gift that she continued the practice throughout his career until just a couple of years ago.

Worried that she was spending a significant amount of her limited income on shipping the gravy to Vermont, he asked her to give him the recipe. "I want to learn to make the gravy like you do," he said, "and it would make things easier for you, too." So she gave him the recipe and he followed it carefully, and the gravy was not great. He watched her

make the gravy so he could do it just like she did. He tried again. The results were not impressive.

In time, McNulty says, he continued to watch and reflect on what he saw. What he learned was this: There is no recipe for love. For his mother, the act of making the gravy was an act of love and devotion. She gave herself to it. She lost herself in it. Things that cannot be written down happen when you lose yourself in your work. He continued, "Sometimes, she even sings to the gravy."

I'd wager a guess that McNulty's mother did not find making the gravy a thing of passion the first time she tried it—or perhaps even the hundredth. She learned over who knows how much time that making the gravy was a representation of herself—that the task had dignity and possibilities beyond her initial recognition of them. She learned to love to make the gravy. She learned to find happiness in giving herself to the work.

Shortly after I heard McNulty tell the story of singing to the gravy, I read a brief article about a baker of bread in Saratoga Springs, New York. For a long while, Michael London was a university professor. He came upon making bread not as a job but as a calling. He is transported when he talks about the complexity of textures in various breads and the immense satisfaction he finds in the labor-intensive process of making loaves of bread by hand, one at a time. Bread, he says, has become his inner path, his medium. Making bread somehow makes him who he ought to be. As he grows, the bread evolves, he explains, and that makes him one with the bread (Heydari, 2002).

This is a metaphor for the second challenge and opportunity we have as teachers—to allow ourselves to be reshaped by what we do, to become one with it.

It is the case that teaching is best when we learn to sing to the gravy, to find ourselves in the labor-intensive process of making bread, one loaf at a time. Through cultivated passion for whom we teach and what we teach, we become what we can be, even as we accept the quixotic challenge of helping every learner we encounter become what they can be.

How do we begin when there is no paved road for us to travel? We just begin. Joan Cone (1993), a high school teacher whose career typifies the teacher who changes course to extend the possibilities of more and more students, reminds us that we learned to ride a bike not by studying about it until we were confident, but by getting on, falling off, and climbing on again. The same might be said for making gravy or kneading bread. We learn by beginning and by keeping on.

Our young, our schools, our country, and our world are better for each teacher who musters up all the courage he or she can find and says to the fox, "Can you show me how to tame you?"

References

Allington, R. (2001). *What really matters to struggling readers: Designing research-based programs*. New York: Longman.

Apple, M., & Beane, J. (1995). *Democratic schools*. Alexandria, VA: Association for Supervision and Curriculum Development.

Ayres, W., Klonsky, M., & Lyon, G. (Eds.) (2000). *A simple justice: The challenge of small schools*. New York: Teachers College Press.

Beane, J. (1990). *Affect in the curriculum: Toward democracy, dignity, and diversity*. New York: Teachers College Press.

Bell, L. (2002–2003). Strategies that close the gap. *Educational Leadership, 60*(4), 32–34.

Billmeyer, R., & Barton, M. (1998). *Teaching reading in the content areas: If not me, then who?* Aurora, CO: McREL. Aurora.

Brimijoin, K., Marquissee, E., & Tomlinson, C. (2003). Using data to differentiate instruction. *Educational Leadership, 60*(5), 70–73.

Burke, J. (2000). *Reading reminders: Tools, tips, and techniques*. Portsmouth, NH: Heinnemann.

Burke, J. (2002). *Tools for thought: Graphic organizers for your classroom*. Portsmouth, NH: Heinemann.

Callahan, C., Tomlinson, C., Reis, S., & Kaplan, S. (2000, June). TIMMS and high ability students: Message of doom or opportunity for reflection? *Phi Delta Kappan*, 787–790.

Campbell, L., & Campbell, B. (1999). *Multiple intelligences and student achievement: Success stories from six schools*. Alexandria, VA: Association for Supervision and Curriculum Development.

Carter, S. (2001). *No excuses: Lessons from 21 high-performing, high-poverty schools*. Washington, DC: The Heritage Foundation.

Center for Immigration Studies (2001). *Immigrants in the U.S.—2000: A snapshot of America's foreign-born population*. Washington, DC: Author.

Chbosky, S. (1999). *The perks of being a wallflower*. New York: Pocket Books.

Clayton, M., & Forton, M. (2001). *Classroom spaces that work*. Greenfield, MA: The Northeast Foundation for Children.

Clyde, J., & Condon, M (2000). *Get real: Bringing kids' learning lives into the classroom*. York, ME: Stenhouse.

Codell, E. (1999). *Educating Esmé: Diary of a teacher's first year*. Chapel Hill, NC: Algonquin Press.

Cohen, E. (1994). *Designing groupwork. Strategies for the heterogeneous classroom* (2nd ed.). New York: Teachers College Press.

Cole, R. (Ed.) (2001). *More strategies for educating everybody's children*. Alexandria, VA: Association for Supervision and Curriculum Development.

Cone, J. (1993). Learning to teach an untracked class. *The College Board Review, 169*. pp. 20–27, 31.

Costa, A., & Kallick, B. (2000). *Discovering and exploring habits of mind*. Alexandria, VA: Association for Supervision and Curriculum Development.

Csikszentmihalyi, M. (1990). *Flow: The psychology of optimal experience*. New York: Harper & Row.

Csikszentmihalyi, M., Rathunde, K., & Whalen, S. (1993). *Talented teenagers: The roots of success and failure*. New York: Cambridge University Press.

Cummings, C. (2000). *Winning strategies for classroom management*. Alexandria, VA: Association for Supervision and Curriculum Development.

Danielson, C. (2002). *Enhancing student achievement: A framework for school improvement*. Alexandria, VA: Association for Supervision and Curriculum Development.

Delpit, L. (1995). *Other people's children: Cultural conflict in the classroom.* New York: The New Press.

Dweck, C. (1986). Motivational processes affecting learning. *American Psychologist, 5,* 1179–1187.

Erickson, H. L. (2002). *Concept-based curriculum and instruction: Teaching beyond the facts.* Thousand Oaks, CA: Corwin.

Finnan, C., & Swanson, J. (2000). *Accelerating the learning of all students: Cultivating culture change in schools, classrooms, and individuals.* Boulder, CO: Westview Press.

Garcia, E. (2002). *Student cultural diversity: Understanding and meeting the challenge.* Boston: Houghton Mifflin.

Gartin, B., Murdick, N., Imbeau, M., & Perner, D. (2002). *Differentiating instruction for students with developmental disabilities in the general education classroom.* Arlington, VA: Council for Exceptional Children.

Gersten, R., Fuchs, L., Williams, J., & Baker, S. (2001). Teaching reading comprehension strategies to students with learning disabilities: A review of research. *Review of Educational Research 71,* 279–320.

Giff, P. (2001). *All the way home.* New York: Delacourt.

Ginsberg, M. & Wlodkowski, R. (2000). *Creating highly motivating classrooms for all students.* San Francisco: Jossey-Bass.

Given, B. (2002). *Teaching to the brain's natural learning systems.* Alexandria, VA: Association for Supervision and Curriculum Development.

Haycock, K. (2001). Closing the achievement gap. *Educational Leadership, 58*(6), 6–11.

Heath, S. (1983). *Ways with words: Language, life, and work in communities and classrooms.* New York: Cambridge University Press.

Heydari, F. (2002, December). Wants and kneads. *USAirways Attache,* p. 24.

Hopfenberg, W., & Levin, H. (1993). *The accelerated schools: Resource guide.* San Francisco: Jossey-Bass.

Howard, P. (1994). *An owner's manual for the brain.* Austin, TX: Leornian Press.

Jensen, E. (1998). *Teaching with the brain in mind.* Alexandria, VA: Association for Supervision and Curriculum Development.

Katz, L., & Chard, S. (1997). *Engaging children's minds: The project approach.* Norwood, NJ: Ablex.

Keefe, C. (1996). *Label-free learning: Supporting learning with disabilities.* York, ME: Stenhouse.

Kiernan, L. (Producer) (2002). *A visit to a differentiated classroom* [Videotape]. Alexandria, VA: Association for Supervision and Curriculum Development.

Kingsolver, B. (1997). *Animal dreams.* New York: Harper Collins.

Kottler, E., & Kottler, J. (2002). *Children with limited English: Teaching strategies for the regular classroom* (2nd ed.). Thousand Oaks, CA: Corwin.

Kriete, R. (2002). *The morning meeting book.* Greenfield, MA: The Northeast Foundation for Children.

Levine, M. (2002). *A mind at a time.* New York: Simon & Schuster.

Levy, S. (1996). *Starting from scratch: One classroom builds its own curriculum.* Portsmouth, NH: Heinemann.

Marzano, R. (1992). *A different kind of classroom: Teaching with dimensions of learning.* Alexandria, VA: Association for Supervision and Curriculum Development.

Maslow, A. (1962). *Toward a psychology of being.* Princeton: Van Nostrand.

McWhorter, J. (2001). *Losing the race.* New York: Perennial.

Meir, D. (1995). *The power of their ideas: Lessons for America from a small school in Harlem.* Boston: Beacon.

National Research Council (1999). *How people learn: Brain, mind, experience, and school.* Washington, DC: National Academy Press.

Nelson, G. (2001, October). Choosing content that's worth knowing. *Educational Leadership, 59*(2), 12–16.

North Carolina Commission on Raising Achievement and Closing Gaps (2001, December). *First report to the State Board of Education.* Raleigh, NC: Author.

Parks, S., & Black, H. (1992). *Organizing thinking: Book I.* Pacific Grove, CA: Critical Thinking Press and Software.

Pavelka, P. (1999). *Create independent learners: Teacher-tested strategies for all ability levels.* Peterborough, NH: Crystal Springs Books.

Phenix, P. (1964). *Realms of meaning.* New York: McGraw-Hill.

Reeves, D. (2002, March/April). Six principles of effective accountability. *Harvard Education Letter,* 7–8.

Saint-Exupery, A. (1971). *The little prince.* New York: Harcourt Brace.

Schlechty, P. (1997). *Inventing better schools: An action plan for educational reform.* San Francisco: Jossey-Bass.

Schoen, S., & Schoen, A. (2002). Action research in the classroom: Assisting a linguistically different learner with special needs. *Teaching Exceptional Children, 35*(3), 16–21.

Schon, D. (1987). *Educating the reflective practitioner.* San Francisco: Jossey-Bass.

Schumm, J., Moody, S., & Vaughn, S. (2000). Grouping for reading instruction: Does one size fit all? *Journal of Learning Disabilities, 33,* 477–488.

Shea, T., & Bauer, A. (1997). *An introduction to special education: A social systems perspective* (2nd ed.). Madison, WI: Brown and Benchmark.

Silver, H., Hanson, J., Strong, R., & Schwartz, P. (1996). *Teaching styles and strategies: Interventions to enrich instructional decision making* (3rd ed.). *Manual #2 in the Unity in Diversity Series.* Woodbridge, NJ: Thoughtful Education Press.

Singleton, G. (2001, December 4). *Breaking the silence: Ushering in courageous conversation about the impact of race on student achievement.* Keynote presentation at the 33rd Annual National Staff Development Council Annual Conference, Denver, CO.

Sizer, T., & Sizer, N. (1999). *The students are watching: Schools and the moral contract.* Boston: Beacon.

Smith, M., & Wilhelm, J. (2002). *"Reading don't fix no Chevys": Literacy in the lives of young men.* Portsmouth, NH: Heinemann.

Sousa, D. (2001). *How the brain learns* (2nd ed.). Thousand Oaks, CA: Corwin Press.

Stephens, H., & Jairrels, V. (2002). Weekend study buddies: Using portable learning centers. *Teaching Exceptional Children, 35*(3) 36–39.

Sternberg, R. (in press). Developing successful intelligence in all children: A potential solution to underachievement in ethnic minority students. In M.C. Wang & R.D. Taylor (Eds.) *Closing the achievement gap.* Philadelphia, PA: The Laboratory for Student Success at Temple University.

Sternberg, R., & Grigorenko, E. (2001). Learning disabilities, schooling, and society. *Phi Delta Kappan, 83,* 335–338.

Sternberg, R., & Grigorenko, Ferrari, M., & Clinkenbeard, P. (1999). A triarchic analysis of an aptitude-treatment interaction. *European Journal of Psychological Assessment, 15*(1), 1–11.

Sternberg, R., Torff, B., & Grigorenko, E. (1998). Teaching triarchically improves student achievement. *Journal of Educational Psychology, 90,* 374–384.

Stiggins, R. (2001). *Student-involved classroom assessment, 3rd edition.* Upper Saddle River, NJ: Merrill Prentice Hall.

Stigler, J., & Hiebert, J., (1999). *The teaching gap: Best ideas from the world's teachers for improving education in the classroom.* New York: The Free Press.

Stronge, J. (2002). *Qualities of effective teachers.* Alexandria, VA: Association for Supervision and Curriculum Development.

Sullivan, M. (1993). *A meta-analysis of experimental research studies based on the Dunn & Dunn learning styles model and its relationship to academic achievement and performance.* Doctoral dissertation, St. John's University, Jamaica, NY.

Taba, H. (1962). *Curriculum and practice.* New York: Harcourt, Brace & World.

Tomlinson, C. (1999). *The differentiated classroom: Responding to the needs of all learners.* Alexandria, VA: Association for Supervision and Curriculum Development.

Tomlinson, C. (2001). *How to differentiate instruction in mixed ability classrooms* (2nd ed.). Alexandria, VA: Association for Supervision and Curriculum Development.

Tomlinson, C., & Allan, S. (2000). *Leadership for differentiating schools and classrooms.* Alexandria, VA: Association for Supervision and Curriculum Development.

Tomlinson, C., Brighton, C., Hertberg, H., Callahan, C., Moon, T., Brimijoin, K., Conover, L., & Reynolds, T. (in press). Differentiating instruction in academically diverse classrooms: A literature review of definitions, rationales, and underpinnings. *Journal for the Education of the Gifted.*

Tomlinson, C., Kaplan, S., Renzulli, J., Purcell, J., Leppien, J., & Burns, D. (2001). *The parallel curriculum model: A design to develop high potential and challenge high-ability learners.* Thousand Oaks, CA: Corwin.

Tompkins, J. (1996). *A life in school: What the teacher learned.* Cambridge, MA: Perseus.

Trumbull, E., Rothstein-Fisch, C., & Greenfield, P., & Quiroz, B. (2001). *Bridging cultures between home and school: A guide for teachers*. Mahwah, NJ: Lawrence Erlbaum.

U.S. Department of Education, National Center for Educational Statistics (2000). *The condition of education*. Washington, DC: Author.

Vygotsky, L. (1962). *Thought and language*. Cambridge, MA: MIT Press.

Vygotsky, L. (1978). *Mind in society*. Cambridge, MA: Harvard University Press.

Wiggins, G., & McTighe, J. (1998). *Understanding by design*. Alexandria, VA: Association for Supervision and Curriculum Development.

Wolfe, P. (2001). *Brain matters: Translating research into classroom practice*. Alexandria, VA: Association for Supervision and Curriculum Development.

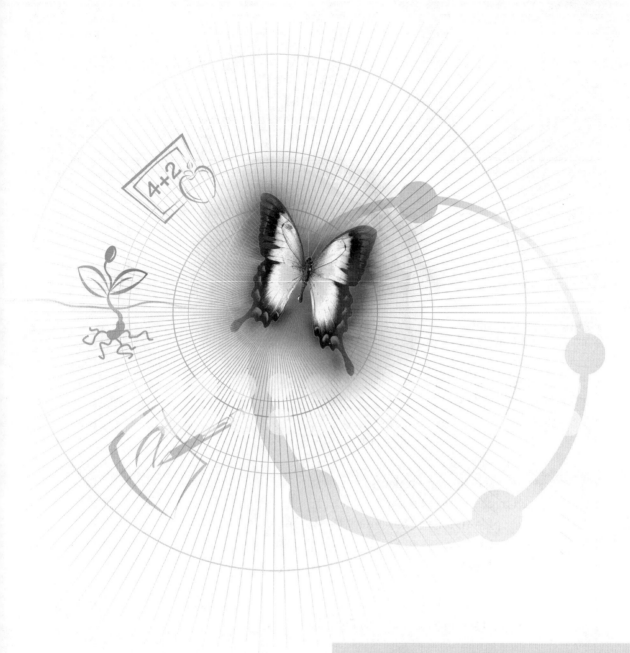

Toolbox

List of Toolbox Figures

FIGURE T.1

Student Profile Survey

Explanation: This is an example of a student profile survey developed by a teacher to help her and her students *begin* to think about their learning preferences and interests.

Directions: *Below are some words that describe how people learn and what people like.*
- *Look at the list and decide which ones REALLY sound like you. Put those in the column on the left.*
- *Look at the list again. Pick out the words that really DON'T sound like you. Put those in the column on the right*
- *There will be some words you don't put in either column because they are a little like you, a little different from you, or you just aren't sure.*
- *Also put in the "like me" column other important things to know about you, your interests, and ways of learning that aren't on the list you were given to pick from.*

Very logical	Like to do one thing at a time	Need quiet when I work
Very creative	Like to do several things at a time	Need noise when I work
Sit still when I learn	Like to work with words	Like collecting things
Wiggle when I learn	Like to work with numbers	Like making things
Like to plan things	Like to work with objects	Like to work alone
Like to be told how to do things	Like music	Like to work with people
Like choices about how to do things	Like art	Like to know the big picture
Great at planning	Not great at planning	Like details

Like Me	Not Like Me

FIGURE T.2

Student Interest Survey

Explanation: This is a second example of a teacher-developed survey to gather information about student interests and learning preferences.

. . . .

ABOUT YOU

Directions: *Please help me know you better so I can teach you better. Give as much information as you can.*

1. What are your favorite things to do outside of school? (Please tell why you like them.)

2. When have you felt really proud of yourself? Please explain why you felt that way.

3. What are you good at in school? How do you know?

4. What's hard for you in school? What makes it hard?

5. What are some ways of learning that work for you?

6. What are some ways of learning that don't work well for you? Why?

7. What's your favorite

- Book _____

- TV show _____

- Movie _____

- Kind of music _____

- Sport _____

8. What are some things you'd really like to learn about?

9. What are some things you really care about getting better in? Why?

10. What else should I know about you as a person and a student that could help me teach you better?

11. Describe how you see yourself as an adult. What will you be doing? Enjoying? Working toward?

FIGURE T.3

Anchor Activity Sheets

Explanation: The following two handouts are examples of anchor activity guides given to students by teachers so students have productive choices when they complete assigned tasks. Similar guides can be developed in any subject and for any grade. They can also be used as homework alternatives when a homework assignment given to some students is inappropriate for others.

What Do I Do If I Finish Early?

When you think you are faced with nothing to do (OH NO—NOT POSSIBLE):

FIRST, ask yourself, "Is there anything else I need to finish?" If the answer is "no," THEN choose something from this list that we brainstormed.

- Practice keyboarding

- Arithmetwists

- Illustrate a story you've written

- Play a quiet math or language game

- Write a morning message for a class

- Practice your cursive or calligraphy

- Read—comics, letters, books, poetry, encyclopedias, etc.

- Help someone else (this is NOT an opportunity to chat)

- Work on an independent study of your choice

- Find out how to say your spelling words in Spanish

- Pick something from the X Factor Volunteer Board to do

- Use your imagination and creativity to challenge yourself

- Write—a letter, poetry in your Writer's Notebook, a story, a comic, etc.

Source: Judy Rex, Scottsdale, AZ. Used with permission.

Writing Bingo

Try for one or more BINGOs this month. Remember, you must have a real reason for the writing experience! If you mail or e-mail your product, get me to read it first and initial your box! Be sure to use your writing goals and our class rubric to guide your work.

Writing
B I N G O

Recipe	Thank you note	Letter to the editor	Directions to one place from another	Rules for a game
Invitation	E-mail request for information	Letter to a pen pal, friend, or relative	Skit or Scene	Interview
Newspaper article	Short story	FREE Your choice:	Grocery or shopping list	Schedule for your work
Advertisement	Cartoon strip	Poem	Instructions	Greeting card
Letter to your teacher	Proposal to improve something	Journal for a week	Design for a Web page	Book—Think Aloud

Source: Adapted from *Managing a Diverse Classroom,* by Carol Cummings, Copyright 1998.

FIGURE T.4

Schedule Chart

Explanation: This is an example of a daily schedule chart used by a teacher to help organize classroom time and to help students work more independently as they learn to follow the schedule. Because the students' names are on clothespins, they can be easily moved to allow flexibility in group composition and size. What students do in a particular task (for example, listening or writing) can vary based on learner interest or need. The teacher can use the schedule with a horizontal row representing five "periods" or blocks in part of a morning, or simply say at a given time, "Boys and girls, we are going to work now on Block No. 4. Please look at our schedule and see where you should go to do your work." Of course the number of options and rotations on a schedule chart can be smaller or larger than the number represented here, and student groups can be smaller or larger as well. Note that in each vertical rotation, the teacher has scheduled herself to work directly with one group of students on a basic skills need (math with the teacher or reading circle).

	1	2	3	4	5
Joey Rachel Tjuan Emerson	Listening	Writing	Read with a Friend	Math	Math with a Teacher
Ilse Li Raphael Cassie	Reading Circle	Art	Handwriting	Word Work	Listening
Jaime Barb Liz William	Writing	Math with a Teacher	Student Choice	Art	Read with a Friend
Wendy Tinesha Franklin Carlos	Student Choice	Handwriting	Reading Circle	Read with a Friend	Word Work
Christopher Nova Jay	Math	Student Choice	Word Work	Reading Circle	Writing
Felissa Jason Serena David	Word Work	Read with a Friend	Math	Listening	Student Choice

FIGURE T.5

Checklists of Student Skills

Explanation: Using skills checklists such as the two that follow make it possible for teachers to assign students varied work and still monitor students' progress as they work to master prescribed skills.

Oral Reading Assessment

Name _____ Teacher _____

Grade _____ Selected by _____

1. Book Title _____ Date _____

2. Book Title _____ Date _____

3. Book Title _____ Date _____

Reading Strategies the Child Uses	Book 1	Book 2	Book 3
Skips unknown word and reads on			
Guesses what the word might be			
Starts over and reads the whole sentence			
Derives meaning from pictures			
Uses beginning letter as a clue			
Asks for help			
Miscues			
Keeps intended meaning (cat, kitten)			
Substitutes phonetically similar words (cat/can)			
Skips words			
Inserts words			
Self-corrects miscues so the text makes sense			

Comprehension	Book 1	Book 2	Book 3
Reads with expression			
Retells the story			
Identifies main idea			

Comments		
Book 1	Book 2	Book 3

Source: Oral Reading Assessment reprinted with permission from *The Multi-Age Classroom* by Bev Maeda (Creative Teaching Press, Inc., Huntington Beach, CA © 1994).

Checklist of Written Expressive Skills

Name _____ Date _____

Age _____ Evaluation No. _____

	Consistent	Inconsistent/ Emerging	Absent	N/A	Comments
Content					
• Ideas contain:					
1. Main idea					
2. Relevant information					
3. Descriptive details					
• Organization contains:					
1. Title					
2. Appropriate introduction					
3. Appropriate sequence					
4. Appropriately sequenced paragraphs					
5. Appropriately sequenced sentences within paragraphs					
Style					
• Intent					
1. Purpose is apparent					
2. Audience is considered					
• Word choice					
1. Correct words used					
2. Precise words used					
3. Variety of words used					
• Sentence structure					
1. Sentences are complete					
2. Sentences are clear					
3. Length varies					
4. Type varies					

	Consistent	Inconsistent/ Emerging	Absent	N/A	Comments
Transcription					
• Syntax					
1. Verb usage					
a. Correct subject/verb agreement					
b. Correct auxiliary verbs					
c. Consistent tense					
2. Pronoun usage					
a. Correct reference					
b. Correct subject/object					
3. Correct adjective/adverb usage					
4. General usage					
a. Correct plural usage					
b. Standard English used					
• Punctuation					
1. End punctuation					
2. Commas					
3. Apostrophes					
• Capitalization					
1. First word					
2. Proper nouns					
3. First person					
4. Titles					
5. First word in quotation					
• Spelling					
1. Uses beginning sounds					
2. Uses letter names					
3. Spells phonetically					
4. Uses traditional spelling					

*N/A = not applicable

Analysis of individual items under each category is optional

Source: Adapted from *Label-Free Learning: Supporting Learners with Disabilities* by Charlotte Hendrick Keese, copyright © 1996, reprinted with permission of Stenhouse Publishers.

FIGURE T.6

Student Checklist for Project Requirements

Explanation: This is an example of a checklist of required components in an upper elementary book-publishing project on the American Revolution. Students use the checklist as they work to make sure they are preparing all the parts of the project. They turn in the checklist with the final product. This is not a rubric to guide thinking about quality; rather, it is simply an inventory of requirements.

Checklist for American Revolution Book

Directions: *As you work with your American Revolution book, use this checklist along with the product description and rubric to help guide you to do complete and high-quality work. A couple of days before the book is due, we'll take a few minutes to let everyone have a friend double check to make sure your work has all the important elements (including proofreading) and to sign your checklist, indicating this is the case. Please be sure you sign as well. You must turn in the checklist along with your final copy of your book.*

Does your final book include:

❑ **Cover**
   ❑ Title
   ❑ Author
   ❑ Graphic that helps readers think about the book

❑ **Title page**
   ❑ Title
   ❑ Author
   ❑ Place of publication

❑ **Table of contents**
   ❑ Chapter titles
   ❑ Page numbers

❑ **Five required chapters**
   ❑ Introduction
   ❑ Background
   ❑ Turning-point event
   ❑ Resolution
   ❑ Looking back and ahead

❑ **Credits for illustrations and tables**
   ❑ Page numbers
   ❑ Reference section
   ❑ Evidence of revision and proofreading

_____

Peer signature indicating a complete review

_____

Author's signature

FIGURE T.7

Example of Rubric

Explanation: Rubrics such as the simple one that follows can be very helpful to students and teachers in assessing learners' current proficiency levels, setting individual goals for upcoming work, and making clear expectations for assignments.

Exemplars Primary Science Rubric

Levels	Science Tools	Science Concepts	Reasoning Strategies	Communication
Getting Started (Novice)	I did not use tools yet.	I don't get it yet.	I mixed up steps.	I did not record or share.
Almost (Apprentice)	I tried to use some tools. Data collection started.	I get some of it.	I'm taking steps.	I started to record and share my ideas.
Got It! (Practitioner)	I did use tools. Most of my data were complete.	I get it.	I organized steps.	I did record and share my ideas.
WOW! (Expert)	Excellent use of all tools. Data collection complete. I can demonstrate.	My ideas shine! I can teach it to a friend.	I made more connections.	I did record details and asked questions.

Source: Copyright © Exemplars Primary Science, 2001

FIGURE T.8

Planning Guide for Students

Explanation: This is a step-by-step planning guide that should be helpful to students who skip steps in trying to get from the introduction of a task to its completion. The example below was used with primary students who were developing a museum to demonstrate their knowledge, understanding, and skill about life under the sea. In this portion of the students' work, the class as a whole decided on criteria for their museum posters, based on what they learned on a trip to a local museum and subsequent examination of exhibit posters for that museum. The teacher is hoping to help some of the students in her class pay more attention to the criteria as they plan. The planning guide completed by students was on a large sheet of paper with ample room for writing and drawing.

Here's My Plan to Guarantee Success

Directions: *Complete this plan to make sure your work is successful.*

Here are the characteristics of a good museum poster written by our class.

Our final posters should

• Look real, like what's in the sea. Be authentic.
• Use several colors that show what life under the sea is like.
• Show at least two plants and animals that are part of a system.
• Have a title that helps visitors to the museum understand the exhibit.
• Be neat and have correct spelling.

Write your plan to make sure you do these things.

1. Here's the first sea animal I'll draw:_____
   Here are important things I'll do to make the animal look real (authentic).

   Here's a plant I'll draw that is an important part of the animal's environment:_____
   _____
   Here are things I'll do to make the plant look real (authentic):

2. Here's the second sea animal I'll draw: _____
   Here are important things I'll do to make the animal look real (authentic):

Here's a plant I'll draw that is an important part of the second animal's environment: _____

Here are things I'll do to make the plant look real (authentic):

3. These are the colors I'll use:

Color	Where	Because
a.		
b.		
c.		
d.		
e.		
f.		
g.		

4. My poster title will be: _____

This is a good title to help people understand our exhibit because _____

_____

_____

_____

_____

5. Here's what I'll do to make sure my final poster looks attractive and neat:

6. Here's what I'll do to make sure my final poster has correct vocabulary and spelling:

FIGURE T.9

Step-by-Step Checklist for Research

Explanation: Step-by-step checklists can effectively scaffold the work of students who have difficulty following directions or sequencing tasks, and when tasks are unfamiliar to students.

1. Topic identified and it is something you are passionate about.

2. Internet search completed.

3. Guiding questions written.

4. Subtopics listed.

5. Web done with guiding question as hub; subtopics as spokes.

6. Web transferred to outline form.

7. Four types of resources located (*Web sites, interviews, museum visits, books*).

8. Notes taken on color-coded cards; sorted by questions.

9. First draft written.

10. Three visuals or illustrations developed.

11. Final draft written.

12. Bibliography completed.

13. Score yourself on the rubric.

14. Reflections guide (below) filled out.

Reflections

• What are the strengths of your piece?

• Describe two things you learned about your topic and guiding questions.

• What did you learn about writing a research report?

• What was especially important or helpful to you as you worked on this project?

• If you could continue working on this project, what would you do?

• What advice would you give to someone else who was working on a similar project?

Source: Adapted from *Winning Strategies for Classroom Management* by Carol Cummings. Association for Supervision and Curriculum Development © 2000.

FIGURE T.10

Concept Wall for an Elementary Classroom

Explanation: These students are studying various countries. The concept of "culture" is a focal point of their study and discussion. The teacher asks students to help her generate possible principles, big ideas, or truths about the concept of culture. Their initial ideas go into the proposal column. As time goes on, students test the proposed principles and accept or reject them based on the evidence that accumulates from their study.

WHAT'S THE BIG IDEA

Concept: Culture

We Propose These Big Ideas (Principles)	We Accept These as Principles	We Reject These as Principles
• *Different cultures have common elements like religion, economics, tradition, and families.* • *Cultural differences can cause conflict.* • *When we understand someone's culture better, we understand that person better.* • *People within a culture belong to different cultures.*	• *A culture shapes the people in it.* • *People shape culture.* • *The geography of a region shapes the culture of a region.*	• *People who speak the same language have the same culture.*

FIGURE T.11
Concept Map

Explanation: A concept map can be of great help to teachers in planning meaningful instruction and to students in understanding how lessons fit together to make meaning.

PATTERNS

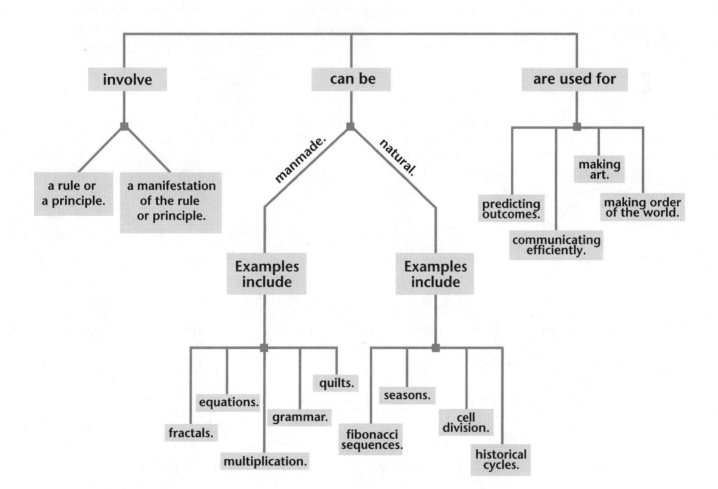

FIGURE T.12

Peer Critique Guide

Explanation: This guide was developed to help middle school students provide feedback on their peers' work in the draft stage of writing image poems. The guide is framed to include goals for the work previously provided for students. In a version prepared for students, the guide would contain space for written comments after each prompt.

Peer Critique Guide For Image Poems

Author _____

Critique partner _____

Poem title _____

Directions: *Please read your partner's poem at least twice before you begin providing feedback. Give your partner detailed responses and suggestions to provide him or her as much "food for thought" as possible. There will be time in class in the next day or two for your partner to ask questions about your ideas.*

1. Describe in your own words the image the poem brings to your mind.

2. What two places do you feel are the strongest in creating an image? Explain why.

3. Where do you feel word choice is most effective? Why?

4. Name all the literary devices the author has used and list each one.

5. Which of the devices work well in helping establish an effective image for you? Why?

6. Which of the devices are less effective in helping establish an image for you? Why?

7. Where might the author give more details to help readers relate to the image? What sorts of information, wording, and so forth would be useful there?

8. Where is the poem too wordy so that the image gets lost in the words? What suggestions do you have for edits there?

9. Overall, where does the poem work least well for you? What suggestions can you give to strengthen that portion of the poem?

10. List or mark on the poem any mechanical errors (for example: spelling errors, punctuation problems, and ragged rhyme).

11. What other suggestions or thoughts about the poem can you give the author that might be helpful in polishing the piece?

FIGURE T.13
Graphic Organizers

Explanation: Graphic organizers such as the three included here are very useful in helping students learn to organize and analyze ideas. They also ensure teacher clarity in planning instruction. Organizers can be used to support students as they read, study, take notes, plan products, and in a variety of other facets of learning.

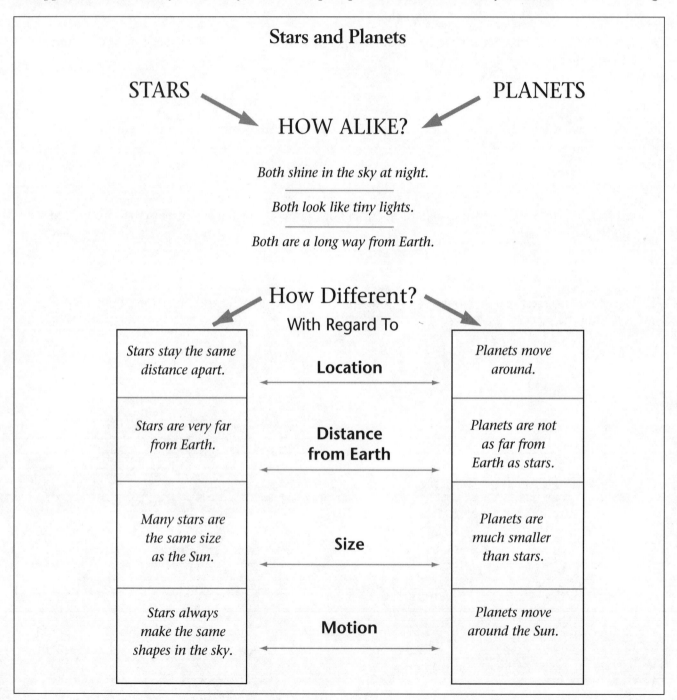

Conversational Roundtable

Name _____ Date_____

Topic_____ Period _____

Suggestions for use: Ask yourself what is the focus of your paper, discussion, or inquiry. Is it a character, a theme, an idea, a country, a trend, or a place? Then examine it from four different perspectives, or identify four different aspects of the topic. Once you have identified the four areas, find and list any appropriate quotations, examples, evidence, or details.

Telemachus

— brave (goes out to look for his father without any knowledge)
— acceptant (accepts the fact that he has to grow up and earn his family's respect)
— sensitive (weeps for father though he barely knows him)
— strong (overcame his childlike fears)
— caring (doesn't want mom to find out he left or she will worry)

Penelope

— cunning (tricks suitors)
— caring (worries about Telemachus after he leaves)
— powerless (has no power to drive away suitors, is a woman)
— remorseful (wishes Odysseus was with her and not gone)
— strong (refuses to marry suitors no matter what)

Character
Q: What kind of people are these characters?

Odysseus

— wise (questions Calypso why he is being set free)
— strong (survives the terrible storm at sea)
— determined (wants to go home with no dawdling)
— faithful (does not marry Nausicaa)
— pleading (both Nausicaa and Aretes give into his cry)
— trusting (trusts Nausicaa to tell him the truth)

Suitors

— disobedient (refuse to leave Odysseus' house)
— stupid (do not realize Penelope is unwinding the rug until they are told)
— disrespectful (make fun of Telemachus for becoming "wise" and "grown-up")
— revengeful (want to kill Telemachus for being so powerful and manly toward them)

There are two main ways by which one can generally tell another person's qualities and ideals. These two ways are by speech and actions. For example, one could say that Penelope is winning because of how she holds off the suitors. Once these tools for recognition are applied, one can more thoroughly grasp the concept of a story.

Source: Reprinted from *Tools for Thought: Graphic Organizers for Your Classroom* by Jim Burke. Copyright © 2002 by Jim Burke. Published by Heinemann, a division of Reed Elsevier, Inc., Portsmouth, NH. Reprinted by permission of the publisher. All rights reserved.

Interactive Notes

Name ___Alive Teregull_____   Date_____

Topic_____   Class/Subject_____

Directions: Use interactive notes to help you read informational or literary texts. Interactive notes guide you through a reading process to help you develop your ideas and express them in academic language. You may put questions, comments, or favorite lines in any column; use the prompts (or create your own) to help you write.

BEFORE Prepare to Read	DURING Question and Comment	AFTER Summarize and Sympathize

• List:
  ☑ Title(s)
  ☑ Headers
  ☑ Subheaders
  ☑ Captions
  ☑ Objectives
  ☑ Themes
  ☑ Words to know
• Ask questions
• Make predictions
• Set a purpose
• Decide what matters most
	• I wonder why …
	• What caused …
	• I think …
	• This is similar to …
	• This is important because …
	• What do they mean by …
	• What I find confusing is …
	• What will happen next is …
	• I can relate to this because …
	• This reminds me of …
	• As I read, I keep wanting to ask …
		• Three important points/ideas are …
		• These are important because …
		• What comes next …
		• The author wants us to think …
		• At this point the article/story is about …
		• I still don't understand …
		• What interested me most was …
		• The author's purpose here is to …
		• A good word to describe this character/this story's tone is … because …
		• The story/idea is similar to …

• Some graduates postpone college for well-paid jobs. • Part-time job at Excite at home. • High-tech detour • Some delay college for high-tech jobs. • People who hold off college to get high-tech jobs. • They want their dream car and a house in the hills. • Cisco Systems networking academy.	• This is about students who put off college to get a job at an Internet company. • Most people can't really get ahead in life with only a high school diploma. • Students get offered $25 an hour as contract employees. • People who don't go to college might miss out on a valuable experience.	• This job might be good to go to part-time and also go to college part-time, but you might be too busy and not get any real free time. • High school graduates go to the Internet jobs and miss out on college or put it off. • People with high school diplomas make $39,799 while people who have a bachelor's degree make $59,048. • But not every student is ready for a four-year college experience after high school.

FIGURE T.14

Evaluation Checklist

Explanation: Checklists are useful for both teacher and students in evaluating how effectively they are interacting with each other. This particular list allows students to review their effect on the communication patterns of their classroom.

When You Work With Peers....

How do you rate in:

1. Making a positive contribution to the work of the group?

1	2	3	4	5
Not Very Good		Okay		The Best!

2. Encouraging the contributions of others?

1	2	3	4	5
Not Very Good		Okay		The Best!

3. Listening to the ideas of others with respect?

1	2	3	4	5
Not Very Good		Okay		The Best!

4. Contributing to high quality?

1	2	3	4	5
Not Very Good		Okay		The Best!

5. Looking for a better way (creativity)?

1	2	3	4	5
Not Very Good		Okay		The Best!

6. Solving problems?

1	2	3	4	5
Not Very Good		Okay		The Best!

7. Disagreeing agreeably?

1	2	3	4	5
Not Very Good		Okay		The Best!

8. Clarifying (goals, roles, directions, expectations, etc.)?

1	2	3	4	5
Not Very Good		Okay		The Best!

9. Using time efficiently and effectively?

1	2	3	4	5
Not Very Good		Okay		The Best!

10. Following directions?

1	2	3	4	5
Not Very Good		Okay		The Best

FIGURE T.15

Developing Clarity About Learning Goals

Explanation: This illustration of how a set of learning goals might look can be posted in the classroom, given to students, or just used by the teacher as a learning guide. The terms for each section mean the following:

- *Know* includes: facts, vocabulary, dates, rules, names of people and places, and other data it's important for students to memorize.
- *Understand* is a statement of principle, truth, or insight that is central to grasping the topic. It is stated in a complete sentence. It often helps in writing understanding statements for the teacher to think, "I want my students to understand that . . . ."
- *Be Able To Do* includes skills. There are several categories of skills that are important for learners. These include *basic skills* (literacy and numeracy); *thinking skills* (such as placing things in order, categorizing, comparing, and providing evidence of a position); *skills of a discipline* (such as graphing in math, showing perspective in art, and map reading in geography); *planning skills* (goal setting, using time effectively, finding and using resource materials effectively, and so forth); and *social skills* (listening, showing empathy, working collaboratively, and so on).

ILLUSTRATION

Topic: Math/Multiplication

Students should know:
Multiplication Tables 1–12.

Students should understand:
- Multiplication is repeated addition.
- If you add the same factor twice, that's x2.
- If you add the same factor three times, that's x3.
- If you add the same factor four times, that's x4, and so on.
- Patterns make math work.
- The patterns in multiplication are predictable.

Students should be able to:
- Repeat the multiplication tables with confidence.
- Explain how multiplication works.
- Multiply two-digit problems correctly.

Two additional examples of Know/Understand/Do frameworks follow. Both are coordinated with Virginia state standards documents, but arranged and augmented to help ensure teacher and student clarity about a unit of study as well as emphasis on central ideas.

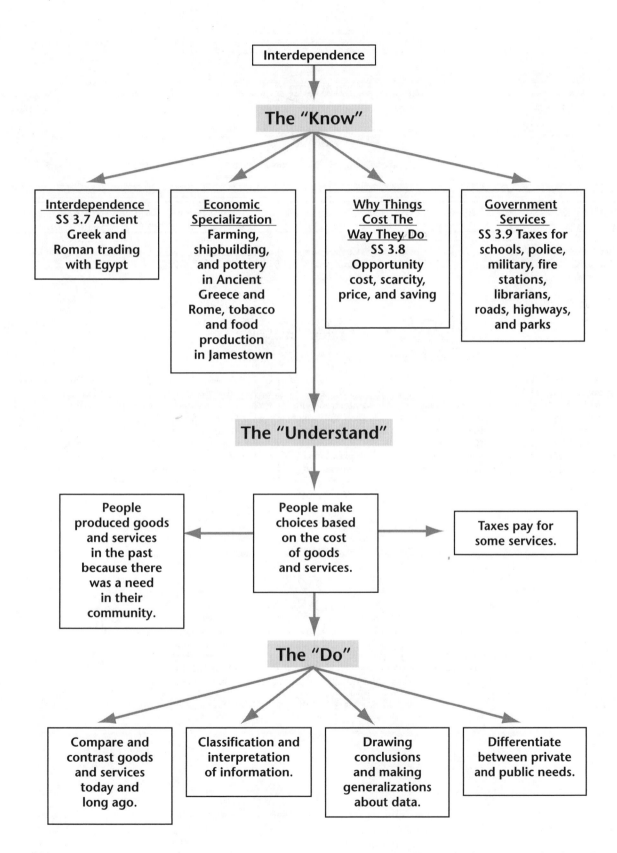

Source: Developed by and reprinted with permission of Kay Brimijoin of Sweet Briar College and Debbie Cooper of Amherst County (Va.) Public Schools, 2000.

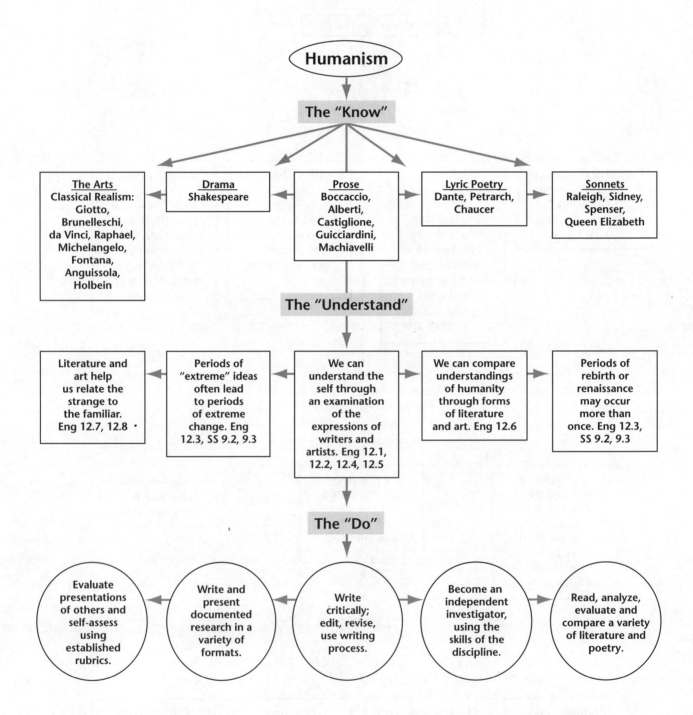

Source: Developed by and used with permission of Cynthia Kelley and Kay Brimijoin.

FIGURE T.16
Learning Menus

Explanation: Learning Menus are designed to give learners choices of tasks, while still ensuring that each learner focuses on knowledge, understanding, and skills designated as essential. A menu assignment may be of short or longer duration. Typically, a menu will include a "main course," which students are required to complete in its entirety; "side dishes," from which students must select a designated number of options; and "desserts," which are optional extension or enrichment tasks.

Menu options can be differentiated in response to student readiness, interest, and learning profile. They are appropriate for all grades and subjects. With older learners, menus might be called "Learning Agendas" with "Imperatives" rather than "Main Courses," "Negotiables" rather than "Side Dishes," and "Options" rather than "Desserts."

To read more about menus, see: Cummings, C. (2000). *Winning strategies for classroom management*. Alexandria, VA: Association for Supervision and Curriculum Development.

MENU EXAMPLE

This menu is designed for elementary science students studying adaptation. It comes about midway in the unit. Students will use class and homework time over a three-day period to complete the menu. As they work, the teacher uses the opportunity to work with students in small groups to assess their understanding of the topic, reteach or extend ideas and skills, and to help students with particular needs related to other topics in the school day. Note that in this example the teacher further differentiates in the Main Course section by designating particular readings appropriate for the student's reading level. Audiotapes of readings can also be used for students who need support in reading or who learn more effectively through aural means. The teacher might also elect to meet early in the menu assignment with students who need reading support and use the opportunity to coach and guide them in reading nonfiction materials. Some students might also benefit from meeting with the teacher to go over the directions, choose tasks, and plan time.

Menu Goals
1. *Students should know*: Adaptation
2. *Students should understand*: Different dinosaurs adapted for different lifestyles and environments.
3. *Students should be able to*:
   - Analyze evidence.
   - Draw conclusions based on evidence.
   - Support conclusions with evidence.

Science Menu on Dinosaurs and Adaptation

Directions: *You will have class time and homework time over the next three days to complete your menu on adaptation. In addition to science time, you may work on your menu when you complete other assigned tasks during the three days. Remember to do your best thinking and writing on the menu. The menu is designed to help you think about how dinosaurs adapted to their particular environments and lifestyles. Look at the principles of adaptation we've been developing as you work. Get your data chart checked by the teacher when you finish all your work in all three sections of the menu.*

Main Course
(You must do everything in this section.)

- Read passages assigned to you on dinosaur legs, feet, claws, and teeth. Your assigned passages are the ones in the _____ folders.

- Complete the data chart as you read to make a good record of what you find out about dinosaur legs, feet, claws, and teeth. This will help you with the rest of your menu work.

- Look at the dinosaur models on the table in the front of the room and complete a prediction/evidence chart for each of the models. On that chart, you'll need to predict how the dinosaur's legs, feet, claws, and teeth point to the kind of lifestyle to which that dinosaur has adapted. You'll also need to give evidence to support your predictions. Use your data chart to help you with evidence. Go back to your assigned passages if you are short of evidence.

Side Dishes
(You must do at least two of these.)

- Go over your prediction and evidence charts with a friend who has completed his or her prediction charts. Write how your ideas are alike and different. Be thorough with your explanations. Put your conclusions in the box on the teacher's desk so she can look over them and discuss them with you.

- Look at a bookmarked Web site on dinosaurs. See if your prediction and evidence charts seem correct based on what you see at the site. On your data chart, write new understandings or evidence about dinosaur adaptation you get from the site. On a green index card, write your name, the Web site you consulted, ways in which the site helps you see your prediction and evidence charts are correct, and ways in which the Web site helps you improve your prediction and evidence charts.

- Watch the dinosaur video set up in the back of the classroom. See if your prediction and evidence charts seem correct based on what you see in the video. On your data chart, write new understandings or evidence about dinosaur adaptation you get from the video. On an orange index card, write your name, ways in which the video helps you see your prediction and evidence charts are correct, and ways in which the video helps you improve your prediction and evidence charts.

- Read more about dinosaurs and adaptation in one or more of the books about dinosaurs on the table in the front of the room. See if your prediction and evidence charts seem correct based on what you read in the books. On your data chart, write new understandings or evidence about dinosaur adaptation you get from the books. On a blue index card, write your name, ways in which the video helps you see your prediction and evidence charts are correct, and ways in which the books help you improve your prediction and evidence charts.

Desserts
(You may do one or more of these if you'd like to.)

- Write a letter from a stegosaurus to kids in the 21st century explaining what life was like for a stegosaurus and how the stegosauri came to be the way they were. Once you have a good draft, put your letter on chart paper, so we can all read it. Since we're assuming the stegosaurus can write (not likely—do you know why?), you can also assume he or she might like to draw and you can illustrate the letter in ways that help us understand what the stegosaurus is saying to us.

- Select a dinosaur that you like. Make and label a sketch that shows us how the dinosaur adapted for his or her particular lifestyle. Assume we don't know much, and make your explanations full enough to teach us.

- Make up a story about a dinosaur that couldn't adapt and what happened as a result. Be sure the story helps us understand how adaptation works—and what would happen if it didn't work! You may tell your story on the tape recorder, so we can listen to it later, or you may write it so we can read it later.

FIGURE T.17

Think-Tac-Toe

Explanation: Think-Tac-Toe, which plays off the familiar childhood game, is a simple way to give students alternative ways of exploring and expressing key ideas and using key skills. Typically, the Think-Tac-Toe grid has nine cells in it like a Tic-Tac-Toe game. The number of rows and cells can, of course, be adjusted. As with related strategies, it's important that no matter which choices students make, they must grapple with the key ideas and use the key skills central to the topic or area of study.

Think-Tac-Toe allows for differentiation by readiness, interest, and learning profile.

THINK-TAC-TOE EXAMPLE

The example that follows was developed as an alternative to book reports in middle school. Rather than having specific content goals, the teacher wanted students to explore characterization, setting, and theme in their novels. This reinforced key concepts students were discussing in their language arts class. The teacher also developed the Think-Tac-Toe to help students make connections between their own lives and the elements of literature.

This example of a Think-Tac-Toe is tiered. That is, while both versions below ask students to explore the concepts of character, setting, and theme in novels of their choice and in their own lives, and while both allow multiple modes of expressing ideas (learning profile differentiation), the first version is somewhat less complex and abstract than the second (readiness differentiation). You'll notice that one item in each row of the second (more advanced) version also appears in the first version. This allowed students who received different versions to work together if they elected to do so. It also blurred distinctions between the two versions. Criteria for student work are also slightly more advanced on the second version. The teacher worked with students to develop descriptors of each of the criteria to help them determine if their work was accurate. Descriptors for "accurate" might include showing where the idea comes from in the book or how faithful it is to the book's theme. Versions are designated on the examples below, but were not noted on student handouts.

At a prescribed time students turned in the Think-Tac-Toe sheet with choices marked, a reading log, and their three pieces of work. Teachers might have students set due dates individually within an appropriate window of time both to accommodate students' schedules and to give teachers more time to provide feedback. It would also work well to have students provide feedback to one another on some or all of the work.

NOVEL THINK-TAC-TOE
(Version 1)

Directions: *Select and complete one activity from each horizontal row to help you and others think about your novel. Remember to make your work*

- *thoughtful.* • *rich with detail.* • *original.* • *accurate.*

Character	Make a pair of collages that compare you and a character in your book in physical and personality traits. Label your collages generously, so viewers understand your thinking.	Write a bio-poem about yourself and another about a main character in the book, so your readers see how you and the character are alike and different. Be sure to include the most important traits in each poem.	Write a recipe or set of directions for how you would solve a problem in your life and another for how a main character in your book would solve a problem. Your list should help us know you and the character better.
Setting	Draw (or paint) and write a greeting card that invites us into the scenery and mood of an important part in the book. Be sure the verse helps us understand what is important in the scene and why.	Make a model or a map of a key place in your life and of an important place in the novel. Find a way to help viewers understand both what the places are like and why they are important in your life and the character's life.	Make two timelines. The first should illustrate and describe at least six to eight shifts in setting in the book. The second should illustrate and explain how the mood changes with the changes in setting.
Theme	Using books of proverbs and quotations, find at least six to eight that you feel reflect what's important about the novel's theme. Find at least six to eight that do the same for your life. Display and explain your choices.	Interview a key character from the book to find out what lessons she thinks we should learn from events in the book. Use a question-and-answer format to present your material. Be sure the interview is meaningful.	Find songs you think reflect an important message from the book. Prepare an audio collage. Write an accompanying card that helps listeners understand why and how you think the songs express the book's meaning. Do the same with your life and its themes.

NOVEL THINK-TAC-TOE

(Version 2)

Directions: *Select and complete one activity from each horizontal row to help you and others think about your novel. Remember to make your work*

> • *insightful.*   • *rich with detail.*   • *accurate.*   • *vivid in imagery and wording.*

Character	Write a bio-poem about yourself and another about a main character in the book, so your readers see how you and the character are alike and different. Be sure to include the most important traits in each poem.	A character in the book is being written about in the paper 20 years after the novel ends. Write the piece. Where has life taken him? Why? Now, do the same for yourself 20 years from now. Make sure both pieces are interesting, feature-type articles.	You're a "profiler." Write and illustrate a full and useful profile of an interesting character from the book with emphasis on personality traits and mode of operating. While you're at it, profile yourself too.
Setting	Research a town or place you feel is equivalent to the one in which the novel is set. Use maps, sketches, and population and other demographic data to help you draw comparisons and contrasts.	Make a model or a map of a key place in your life and of an important place in the novel. Find a way to help viewers understand both what the places are like and why they are important in your life and the character's life.	The time and place in which people find themselves and in which events happen shape those people and events in important ways. Find a way to convincingly prove that idea using the book—and your own life.
Theme	Find out about famous people in history or current events whose experiences and lives reflect the essential themes of your novel. Show us what you've learned.	Create a multimedia presentation that fully explores a key theme from the novel. Use at least three media (for example, music, painting, poetry, sculpture, photography, and calligraphy) in your exploration. Draw at least two comparisons or contrasts between themes in your life and in the novel.	Find several songs you think reflect an important message from the book. Prepare an audio collage. Write an accompanying card that helps listeners understand why and how you think the songs express the book's meaning. Do the same with your life and its themes.

FIGURE T.18
RAFT Activities

Explanation: RAFT is an acronym for Role, Audience, Format, and Topic. In a RAFT, students take on a particular role, develop a product for a specified audience in a particular format and on a topic that gets right at the heart of what matters most in a particular segment of study. At some points, a teacher may want to assign students particular RAFTs and at other points may want the student to make the choice. RAFT assignments are typically of fairly short duration and can be completed at school or at home.

RAFTs offer teachers great flexibility to plan for student readiness, interest, and learning profile. To read more about RAFTs, see: Billmeyer, R. and Barton, M. (1998). *Teaching reading in the content areas: If not me, then who?* Aurora, CO: McREL.

RAFT EXAMPLE 1

This RAFT is designed to be used by students in a French I class as they are developing the basic structure of the language and basic vocabulary sets. Of particular interest here are present tense verbs and vocabulary centered on leisure activities.

RAFT Goals

Students should know

- Names of French-speaking countries.
- Basic geographic features of those countries.
- Conjugation of present tense verbs.
- Vocabulary for leisure time activities.

Students should understand

- How a country's geography affects how its people spend their leisure time.

Students should be able to

- Research a French-speaking country to determine its basic geography.
- Predict leisure activities people in a particular country might enjoy based on its geography.
- Communicate information about leisure activities in French.

Leisure Activities RAFT

Directions: *First, select a French-speaking country from the list on the board. Next, use research materials on the bookshelf, Internet, and in your textbook to find information on the geography of that country. Get as much information about the country's geography as you can find. For example: What is the temperature like in the various seasons? Does it have lakes? Are parts of it bordered by oceans? Are there mountains? What resources are in the country that might affect leisure? Is there something in the history of the country that shapes recreation (for example, a long-time love of music)?*

Then, select one of the following options to help you practice making French sentences that use present tense verbs and vocabulary related to leisure. When you finish your work, we'll do two more things. First, you'll have a chance to go over your work with a classmate to find ways to make it stronger. Second, you'll share what you have done with students who researched other French-speaking countries.

Role	Audience	Format	Topic
Student	Self	Packing list with notes	Here's what I need for my vacation and why I need it.
Native of the country	A visiting athlete	Map with symbols	Here's what to look for and do on your vacation here.
Tourist	Family at home	Series of post cards	Please send my _____ because . . . .
Native of the country	Visitors on vacation	List of do's and don'ts	When in Rome . . . .
Hiker or driver	Roads	Magazine interview	Where are you taking me?
Bureau of Tourism	Potential inhabitants	Travel posters with narration	You'll enjoy our best features!
Radio announcer	Listener	Informational feature	Come share the wonder!
Fill in your	**choice here.**	**Check with the**	**teacher for approval.**

Source: Developed by and used with permission of Cindy A. Strickland, University of Virginia.

RAFT EXAMPLE 2

This RAFT is designed for students in a second grade class as they are learning about endangered and extinct animals in science and about natural resources in social studies. Students study both topics for a number of days before they do the RAFT. This activity serves as a culmination to this period of study.

RAFT Goals

Students should know

- The basic needs of plants and animals.
- The role of natural resources in the lives of people and animals.

Students should understand

- Our actions affect the balance of life on Earth.
- Animals become endangered or extinct when the natural resources they need are damaged or limited.
- Natural resources are not unlimited and must be used wisely.

Student should be able to

- Identify causes of problems because of misuse of natural resources.
- Propose a useful solution to the problems.

RAFT Activity

Directions: *Pick one of these three activities to show what you know about why taking care of natural resources is important to the balance of life in our world. Use what you have learned about our endangered and extinct animals and natural resources to make your work helpful to everyone who sees it. Be ready to explain how you know your work is of high quality.*

Role	Audience	Format	Topic
The Earth	Aliens who might want to live on earth	A written set of rules with reasons	What you need to know and do if you want to live here
An endangered animal	Humans	A poster with an exhibit card to explain it	Why I need you and how you can help save me
A natural resource	Our class	A speech	What people need to know about using this well and why that matters anyhow

Source: Developed by and used with permission of Debby Bulak.

FIGURE T.19

Tiering

Explanation: Tiering is an instructional approach designed to have students of differing readiness levels work with essential knowledge, understanding, and skill, but to do so at levels of difficulty appropriately challenging for them as individuals at a given point in the instructional cycle. To tier an activity or work product:

- Clearly establish what students should know, understand, and be able to do as a result of the activity or product assignment.
- Develop one activity or product assignment that is interesting and engaging for students, squarely focuses on the stated learning goals, and requires students to work at a high level of thought. It's a good idea to begin with an advanced level activity, because doing so is likely to raise the teacher's sights for other learners as well. It is also possible to start with a version of the activity or product that teacher and students have used successfully in the past.
- Think about the readiness levels of students in the class based on pre-assessment, ongoing assessment, and continually growing teacher knowledge of students' general skills levels (in reading, writing, math—or whatever skills are fundamental to the subject at hand).
- Develop enough versions of the original task or product assignment to challenge the range of learners. You may need to create one, two, three, or four additional versions.
- To create multiple versions of a task at different degrees of difficulty, refer to following graphic "The Equalizer" and ensure that the versions for students who continue to struggle with the ideas and skills the task calls for are more foundational, concrete, simple, have fewer dimensions, and so on. To increase the degree of difficulty of a task, move one or more of The Equalizer buttons to the right (making the task more transformational, abstract, complex, multifaceted, and so on).

Continual Assessment and Adaptation
The Equalizer

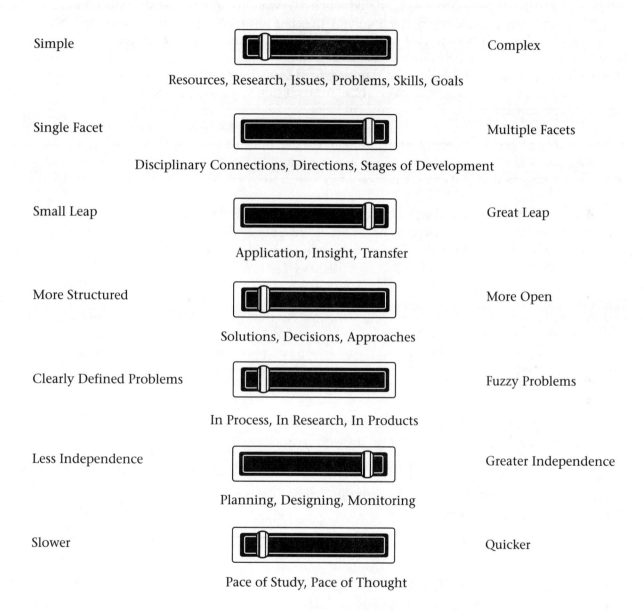

Simple   Complex

Resources, Research, Issues, Problems, Skills, Goals

Single Facet   Multiple Facets

Disciplinary Connections, Directions, Stages of Development

Small Leap   Great Leap

Application, Insight, Transfer

More Structured   More Open

Solutions, Decisions, Approaches

Clearly Defined Problems   Fuzzy Problems

In Process, In Research, In Products

Less Independence   Greater Independence

Planning, Designing, Monitoring

Slower   Quicker

Pace of Study, Pace of Thought

For more information on tiering and The Equalizer, see Tomlinson, C. (1999). *The differentiated classroom: Responding to the needs of all learners.* Alexandria, VA: Association for Supervision and Curriculum Development. Excellent examples of tiered math lessons are available from Exemplars at 271 Poker Hill Road, Underhill, VT 05489 or www.exemplars.com.

TIERED EXAMPLE 1

The kindergarten teacher who used this tiered center was working with all her students on counting. They did many activities every day involving the class in varied approaches to counting. She also wanted to see what her students would do with individual counting tasks at their math center, in which student tasks are tiered based on current skill development. To ensure that students could handle directions at centers, the teacher routinely used several strategies. She went over directions with students orally. She wrote directions at the center, using icons or pictures when possible. She tape-recorded directions. She also used student helpers, who helped anyone who got stuck.

For this tiered task, the center had three levels of counting work—all similar in how they approach using the skill of counting but at different levels of demand. Colors were used to indicate the three levels. Students found their name on a chart, looked for the color beside their name, and did the task on a card of that color. Tape recorders were also color coded to match directions to appropriate tasks.

Once students completed their work, the teacher met with all students whose work was coded with the same color. They shared ideas with one another. She probed and pushed their thinking and gave them things to think about when they went back to the center the next day. When she saw that a student was ready to change colors (that is, levels), she changed the assignment chart. Many students stayed at a particular level for several days before moving. The center stayed in place for about two weeks.

In the example below, degree of difficulty increases as the teacher adds more facets to the tasks and also as the tasks become more abstract (dealing with things not present is more abstract than dealing with things the students can see). Tier 3 has the more complex demand that students not only explain their reasoning but also prove their answer is correct.

Tier 1
- Find a way to count and show how many students are in our class today.
- Be ready to tell how you found out the answer.

Tier 2
- Find a way to count and show how many students are in our class today.
- Count how many are absent today.
- Be ready to tell how you found your answers.

Tier 3
- Find a way to count and show how many girls are in our class today.
- Count and show how many girls are absent today.
- Count and show how many boys are here today.
- Count and show how many boys are absent today.
- Be ready to prove you are right.

TIERED EXAMPLE 2

The teacher of this Spanish I class worked with her students early in the year on vocabulary for basic parts of the human body. They had already worked with numbers in Spanish. In addition, their skills in forming simple Spanish sentences were developing. She wanted the students to practice vocabulary related to body parts, to work orally with a peer, and to practice very simple sentence structures. She began developing her activity with an idea from *Enhancing Foreign Language Instruction in Your Classroom* by Barbara Snyder, modifying and tiering the initial idea.

Students worked in pairs chosen by the teacher based on pre-assessment of student proficiency with the particular vocabulary and formation of simple sentences. Each student received a handout with 15-20 hand-drawn images of aliens from outer space. While alike in basic shape and form, the aliens had different numbers of arms, legs, feet, noses, mouths, eyes, and so on. Two nice features of this task are

1. The teacher provided a support system to enable struggling students to work with a target-level task, rather than reducing task difficulty; and
2. After the activity, the class came together as a whole to share in an interesting culmination to their work. At this point, all students had participated in the same activity.

Target-Level Students

- *Student A selects one of the aliens without telling Student B the choice.*
- *Student B asks questions in an attempt to figure out which alien Student A selected.*
- *Questions must be answerable with a "yes" or "no"—for example, "Does your alien have three eyes"? When Student A answers a question, he or she must do so in a complete sentence—for example, "No, my alien does not have three eyes."*
- *When Student B figures out which alien Student A selected, they trade roles and begin the question-and-answer sequence again.*

Struggling Students

For students who need additional support to succeed at the target task, the teacher does one of the following:
- *Provides a list of possible questions in Spanish,*
- *Provides a list of helpful vocabulary,*
- *Spends the first few minutes of the exercise working with a group of students to help them become familiar and comfortable with the task and its requirements, providing questions or vocabulary, if that seems necessary.*

Advanced Students

In addition to asking questions about the numbers of particular body parts on the alien, Student B (and then Student A) also asks questions about why the alien is formed as it is—for example, "Does your alien have more mouths to eat more?" Student A (and then student B) must respond in a complete sentence—for example, "No, my alien does not eat much." At the end, students write brief statements about the structure and function of the two aliens.

Whole Class

When students finish the tiered activity, the teacher asks each student to design an alien of his own but with the name of the student on the back of the picture rather than the front. She posts all the pictures in the class, and members of the class take turns asking classmates yes/no questions about their aliens to figure out who drew a given picture—for example, "Juan, does your alien have six feet?" Again, the student who is asked the question must respond in a complete sentence.

Source: Developed by and used with permission of Ellie Gallagher, Treasure Mountain Middle School Park City, UT.

FIGURE T.20

Complex Instruction

Explanation: Complex Instruction is a collaborative instructional strategy developed by Elizabeth Cohen at Stanford University. Its purpose is to have students work together in heterogeneous groups on tasks that genuinely draw upon the skills of each of them. A goal of a Complex Instruction task is to ensure that each student is indispensable to the work of the group as a whole. A good Complex Instruction assignment is likely to have the following characteristics:

- Tasks are open ended.
- Tasks are interesting to the students.
- Tasks are fuzzy—can be accomplished in more than one way.
- Tasks are challenging.
- Tasks call upon a wide range of talents, interests, and intelligences used in a real world way.
- Multilingual groups must contain bilingual students to bridge language for peers just learning English, and materials must be available in the languages represented.
- Reading and writing are integrated into the work.
- Tasks involve the use of real objects.
- The teacher moves among groups as they work, asking questions, probing decisions, and facilitating understanding.
- The teacher consistently looks for genuine student strengths and contributions, pointing them out to the class and explaining why the skills and contributions are important.
- Over time the teacher increasingly delegates to students responsibility for learning, ensuring they gain the skills to manage the responsibility effectively.

For more information on Complex Instruction, see Cohen, E. (1994). *Designing groupwork: Strategies for the heterogeneous classroom* (2nd ed.). New York: Teachers College Press.

COMPLEX INSTRUCTION EXAMPLE

This Complex Instruction task is designed for students in a fourth grade class in a state with high stakes testing. They are responsible for learning the history and geography of their state as part of the social studies curriculum. The teacher wanted to introduce the study of Virginia history and geography in a way that helped students see the purpose and liveliness of what they were learning and in ways that helped them learn to appreciate the abilities their peers could bring to a complex task. She assigned students to groups of five and gave each group the following six task cards. When students requested help or information with a particular term or skill, she provided appropriate materials and miniworkshops. She found the students much more eager to learn about the topics and skills when they saw a need for them. The teachers helped the students develop a work plan so that students could specialize in particular tasks, but continue to collaborate with their whole group as they made discoveries, encountered questions, and shared findings. Note that all students are responsible for explaining all tasks.

As the activity ended, the teacher asked each group to present a specific task they had completed and then led the class in a discussion of other findings and questions on that task.

The standards-based learning goals for the Complex Instruction activity follow. Understandings were drawn largely from National Geographic's standards for geography.

Students should know
- Essential vocabulary (legend, latitude, longitude, Mid-Atlantic Region, Atlantic Ocean).
- Geographic regions of Virginia (e.g., Tidewater, Piedmont).
- Key features of each Virginia region.

Students should understand
- Locations of places can be described using terms that show relationships.
- Locations of places can be described using reference systems on maps.
- Reasons can be identified for locations of places.
- Relationships within places include how people depend on the environment.
- Places may be represented and described in many different ways.

Students should be able to
- Read basic maps.
- Use and make map symbols.
- Infer and draw conclusions.
- Use research to achieve understanding.
- Develop an effective work plan.
- Write to show understanding.
- Collaborate effectively.

Directions: *You'll soon be on your way to learning more about Virginia than many adults know. Here's a way to start becoming experts. This task is designed to draw on the strengths and talents of everyone in your group. Six task cards will help you know what to do. Everyone in your group must be ready to explain what your group did with all six tasks and why.*

Task Card 1

Give as many ways as you can to locate Virginia (for example, where it is in relation to bodies of water, to continents, to other states, within the United States, and so on). Find an interesting and useful way to show us all you can figure out about Virginia's location.

Task Card 2

Use reference systems (like numbered grids, latitude, longitude, parallels, and meridians) to locate Virginia precisely on globes and maps. Create a set of instructions we can use to locate Virginia as you did. Assume we know nothing about using globes and maps.

Task Card 3

Draw or sketch places in Virginia with large populations. Create symbols for a map that helps us figure out why so many people live in those places. Post the symbols on a blank map. Make a legend to help us interpret the symbols. Do the same with great Virginia places for recreation.

Task Card 4

Find four cities or towns in Virginia where important or famous people once lived. Have each of those people talk to us about that place, what it was like to be there, how they influenced the place, and how the place influenced them. You can use acted, tape recorded, or video recorded presentations to do this.

Task Card 5

Select one of the people in Task Card 4 and complete a Now and Then chart to show what the following things were like in that person's town when they lived there and what they would be like now: transportation, recreation, population size, important ways of making a living, important resources, life span, and ways of communicating. It's fine to draw and write on the chart.

Task Card 6

Interview someone who has lived in our town for a long time. Find out what has changed, what has stayed the same, what seems better, what seems worse, interesting things the person has done while they've lived here, and other things you think are important for us to know. Get the person to tell you a story about something that happened here. Find a way to help us get to know this person and this town through the eyes of this person.

FIGURE T.21
Task-Specific and Generic Rubrics

Explanation: Rubrics are guides designed to help students think more clearly about the characteristics of quality work. Generally, they delineate important elements of tasks and how those elements look in a progression from stellar to less well developed (or less well developed to stellar, depending on how the rubric is set up).

Often rubrics are subject or task specific. That is, they help students plan and evaluate a particular piece of work. Example 1, which follows, is this sort of rubric. It is an excellent example from a middle school art teacher, one carefully matched to standards and a particular product assignment.

Rubrics can also be more generic, however. That is, they can be developed in ways that allow their use repeatedly during a course or year. Example 2 is a more generic rubric that can be used throughout the year by students in a variety of subjects or repeatedly in a single subject. In this instance, the teacher and students added to the rubric as they developed skills individually and as a group. Example 2 is designed for the middle grades, but could be easily adapted for younger or older students. Example 3 is also a generic rubric. It is designed with elementary students in mind, but could again be adapted for other ages. Its goal is to help students assess their general work habits.

You'll note that Example 1 is set up so that it first displays the most advanced level of production and moves finally to a description of work that is "acceptable." Note, too, that the teacher has not placed quality labels over the cells. That is purposeful, because she realizes that what is excellent for one student at a given point in time may not represent excellence for another. She often "cuts and pastes" the rubrics, giving students one or two columns that are at and just beyond the student's current working level. The student plans work and sets goals by circling descriptors in the columns for which he or she will strive during a project. Thus, students are working to improve themselves rather than competing with others.

The second example begins with "acceptable" work and moves toward more advanced quality. Note that cells have space for teacher and students to add personal goals. Again, specific designations or names for level of quality are left off the grid to allow for focus on individual growth, while still making available a continuum of quality.

Example 3, like the first, moves from highest quality to work that is not yet fully developed.

Rubric Example 1: Illustration

Sketching/Brainstorming	Reads and has a strong understanding of the text to be illustrated and knows the audience. Explores possible interpretations of the text. Brainstorms a variety of ideas and styles (e.g., art deco, realism, impressionism) or uses a different perspective (e.g., serial, eye level). Creates strong, elaborative, thought-provoking sketches. Obtains feedback from peers or instructor on ideas. Knows illustration is communicating intended idea.	Reads and has a strong understanding of the text to be illustrated and knows the audience. Finds a few possible interpretations of the text. Brainstorms a variety of ideas and styles (e.g., art deco, realism, impressionism). Creates strong, thought-provoking sketches. Obtains feedback from peers or instructor on ideas. Feels strongly that illustration is communicating intended idea.	Reads and has an understanding of the text to be illustrated and knows the audience. Looks for a few possible interpretations of the text. Brainstorms a variety of ideas. Creates three strong varied sketches. Obtains feedback from peers or instructor on ideas. Feels that illustration is communicating intended idea.	Reads and has an understanding of the text to be illustrated and knows the audience. Looks for more than one possible interpretation of the text. Brainstorms a variety of ideas. Creates three strong sketches. Obtains feedback from peers on ideas. Feels that illustration is communicating intended idea.
Style and Media Choice	Mindful of audience and meaning of the text when choosing a style of illustration. Communicates mood and tone powerfully—style and images work successfully with the tone of the piece. Insightful choices of style and format that extend the viewer's understanding and enhances the meaning of the text. Chooses a style of shading that creates contrast and interest.	Thoughtful of audience and meaning of the text when choosing a style of illustration. Strongly communicates mood and tone—style and images work successfully with the tone of the piece. Discerning choices of style and format that extend the viewer's understanding and enhances the meaning of the text. Chooses a style of shading that creates contrast and interest.	Aware of audience and meaning of the text when choosing a style of illustration. Clearly communicates mood and tone—style and images work very well with the tone of the piece. Perceptive choices of style and format that extend the viewer's understanding of the text. Chooses a style of shading that creates contrast and interest.	Aware of audience and meaning of the text when choosing a style of illustration. Communicates mood and tone—style and images work well with the tone of the piece. Insightful choices of style and format that extend the viewer's understanding of the text. Chooses a style of shading that creates contrast and interest.
Principles of Design	Plans carefully—shows a vast understanding and skillful use of the elements and principles of design. Principles of design are used effectively to clearly convey meaning and amplify what the artist is communicating to the viewer. Creative and unconventional use of space. Text integrated in an original and interesting way.	Plans carefully—shows a strong understanding and skillful use of the elements and principles of design. Principles of design are used effectively to convey meaning and enhance what the artist is communicating to the viewer. Creative and original use of space. Text integrated in a new an interesting way.	Plans carefully—shows an understanding and uses successfully many of the elements and principles of design. Principles of design are used effectively to convey meaning and enhance what the artist is communicating to the viewer. Creative and original use of space. Text is integrated in an interesting way.	Plans carefully—shows an awareness of and uses well many of the elements and principles of design. Principles of design are used to convey meaning and enhance what the artist is communicating to the viewer. Creative and original use of space. Integrates text successfully.

(continues)

Rubric Example 1: Illustration *(continued)*

Craftsmanship	Exhibits mastery of pen and ink media and shows value contrast through striking shading techniques. Displays exemplary craftsmanship—work is free of smudges and preliminary pencil drawings—each mark is purposeful. Work is also free of wrinkles and other signs of wear.	Exhibits skillful execution of pen and ink media and shows a value contrast through strong shading techniques. Displays virtually flawless craftsmanship—work is free of smudges and preliminary pencil drawings—each work is purposeful. Work is also free of wrinkles and other signs of wear.	Exhibits knowledge of pen and ink media and shows value contrast through good shading techniques. Displays strong craftsmanship—work is virtually free of smudges and preliminary pencil drawings—each mark is purposeful. Work is also free of wrinkles and other signs of wear.	Exhibits competency in pen and ink media and shows value contrast through shading technique. Displays good craftsmanship—work is mostly free of smudges and preliminary pencil drawings—each mark is purposeful. Work is mostly free of wrinkles and other signs of wear.
Creativeness and Originality	Deals with meaning in a broad and universal way. Challenges conventions (challenges the way we do, see, think about things, or in the use of the materials). Evokes emotions (or humor if appropriate). Employs risk-taking. Is insightful and surprising. Extends audience's understanding of the text.	Deals with meaning in a broad way. Challenges some conventions (challenges the way we do, see, think about things, or in the use of materials). Evokes emotions (or humor if appropriate). Employs risk-taking. Is insightful. Extends audience's understanding of the text.	Deals with meaning in a new and interesting way. Evokes emotions (or humor if appropriate). Employs risk-taking. Is insightful. Extends audience's understanding of the text.	Deals with meaning in a new way. Evokes emotion (or humor if appropriate). Employs risk-taking. Is insightful. Extends audience's understanding of the text.

Source: Used by permission of Melissa K. Valentine, Smith Middle School, Chapel Hill, NC.

Rubric Example 2: A Generic Rubric

Quality of Thought	• Poses and seeks answers to important questions. • Uses logical progression of thought. • Supports ideas with evidence.	• Balances big picture with detail. • Draws valid & supported conclusions from evidence. • Makes useful connections. • Shows evidence of self-aware thought. • Elaborates thoughts effectively.	• Looks at ideas from varied viewpoints. • Makes unexpected and important connections. • Shows insight. • Seeks creative approaches. • Shows self-regulation of thought, depending on purpose
Quality of Research	• Uses appropriate range of resources. • Gives credit appropriately. • Accurately captures key ideas & issues. • Makes ideas their own. Doesn't copy. • Carefully logs research processes & sources.	• Screens resources for most valid or valuable options. • Effectively blends ideas from several sources. • Sees patterns and themes in research.	• Weighs evidence for positions from varied views and sources. • Makes and supports generalizations that show depth of understanding. • Raises questions that point to next level of research.
Quality of Expression	• Develops a clear flow of ideas—easy to follow. • Uses effective beginning, developed middle, sound conclusion. • Uses appropriate vocabulary. • Shows work with mechanics.	• Varies sentence structure effectively. • Uses effective transitions. Beginning catches audience's attention. Middle well elaborated and supported. End captures essence of piece and "punches" key point(s). • Uses powerful word choices. • Shows care & accuracy with mechanics.	• Shows development of own voice. • Seems genuinely to care about ideas and issues. • Effectively uses imagery and figures of speech. • Uses sophisticated, professional-like language.
Habits of Mind	• Thinks before acting. • Asks questions to achieve understanding. • Evaluates own work according to established criteria. • Listens to ideas of others. • Improving with persistence.	• Asks probing questions. • Is aware of and reflects own thinking processes. • Applies knowledge to new situations. • Persists with tasks despite difficulty. • Proposes criteria to improve own work.	• Shows appreciation, awe, or wonder with learning. • Adjusts thinking and work appropriately for task or situation. • Respects perspectives different from own. • Seeks quality more than comfort or ease. • Is highly invested and absorbed in work.

Rubric Example 3: Self-Assessment Rubric for Work Habits

Dimension	Exemplary	Developed	Emerging	Undeveloped
Focus and Good Concentration *(To what extent do you give your full attention to the work being done?)*	I am keenly focused and/or listening closely to whoever is speaking. I do this without adult supervision or reminders. I do not distract others.	I show interest in the task at hand. I rarely distract others, and need minimal supervision or reminders.	I am sometimes distracted or I may distract others, but I respond immediately to reminders by an adult.	I am easily distracted, and often off task. I often distract others from the task at hand. I do not respond positively to peer or adult reminders.
Application of Learning *(To what extent do you apply what you have learned to other classes and to real-life situations?)*	I can explain clearly how to apply what I am learning to real-life situations, and can give examples or demonstrations of those applications. I can identify skills independently and transfer them to real-life situations.	I can explain clearly how to apply what I am learning to real-life situations, and can transfer skills to those situations that were identified for me by an adult.	I can explain how to apply what I am learning to real-life situations and give examples, but I am unable to demonstrate the application.	I am unable to explain or demonstrate real-life applications of material presented in class.
Persistence *(To what extent do you work toward continuous improvement without giving up?)*	I take charge and maintain ownership of my own learning. I work toward continuous improvement and I am open to any help offered, conscientiously choosing how to use that advice. I do not give up, even if the task becomes difficult at times.	I can work conscientiously toward improvement and seek help when experiencing difficulty (prior to the point of failure). I require little encouragement to keep trying.	I work toward improvement when directed to do so, but I need consistent encouragement. I seek help when experiencing failure or when advised to do so. I need a lot of encouragement and prodding to keep trying.	I demonstrate little interest in improvement. I give up easily and do not seek help when I need it or when advised to do so. I do not respond to encouragement and rarely act on given advice or help. Sometimes, I give up without really trying at all.
Independent Thinking *(To what extent are you willing to think through problems independently?)*	I demonstrate a willingness to think on my own; I see problems as creative opportunities to use and apply learned thinking skills and processes. I apply these skills and processes effectively and appropriately as needed.	I am willing to think independently with the support of an adult. I can identify when there is a problem to overcome. I attempt to solve those problems using thinking skills and processes I have learned. I need to get support often to do this.	I mostly rely on adult directions and often don't risk thinking for myself in problem situations. I see problems as "risky" and even though I have learned skills for solving problems, I don't apply them independently.	I rely on an adult most of the time to direct me to what needs to be done. I don't often think on my own and I don't choose to solve problems unless I am told to do so. Learned skills and processes are not applied independently.

FIGURE T.22
Learning Contracts

Explanation: A learning contract is a means of providing practice for learners based on their particular learning needs as those needs relate to overall learning goals. Contracts take many different forms and are used in a great range of ways. In general, learning contracts include

- Clarification of learning goals for a unit or topic of study;
- Assessment of learner proficiency with those goals to determine learning needs;
- A "package" of tasks, activities, meeting times with the teacher, and other components likely to help the student continue to develop essential knowledge, understanding, and skills;
- Directions for how the student is expected to work during the contract time, a timeline for completing work, instruction on how to get work approved when it is finished and where to turn it in, and criteria for grading; and
- The actual tasks a student is expected to complete as part of the contract.

CONTRACT EXAMPLE

The following example of a contract was developed by an elementary teacher during a unit of study when it became evident to her that her students were "all over the place" in their understanding and skill regarding math topics they had recently explored. She developed the contract in the shape of a ticket, and students got their ticket punched whenever they successfully completed a particular task. Successful completion of a task was noted by the teacher or a designated student "checker." While everyone's ticket looked alike, different students might have differing assignments under the common headings or topics on the ticket. Note that each student has a time to meet with the teacher (Teacher Feature).

When a teacher knows a student finds the number of parts to an assignment confusing, the teacher can allow that student to select between two activities at a time, glue the choice on the ticket, and move through other tasks in that fashion. Similarly, the teacher can provide timelines for work completion to those students who do not yet plan their own time efficiently. Contracts also lend themselves very well to students with Individual Education Plans, who may need to work on different skills than many of their classmates.

Directions: *We have been working hard on a number of important topics in math. Right now, different students need different kinds of practice to keep growing with the topics. To make sure everyone gets the practice and help he or she needs to be comfortable with the topics, each student has a Math Ticket to complete in the next four days. We will work on the tickets in math time. You can also work on them as an anchor activity when you finish other work. Your ticket will also be your math homework during the next four days.*

To be successful with your contract:
- Sit where you can work hard and concentrate.
- Pay attention to your own contract.
- Help your friends when they get stuck, as long as helping doesn't cause you to get behind in your work.
- When you finish a part of your ticket, bring it to the teacher or a student who is a checker for that task.

- If your task is done correctly, you will get your ticket punched in that place. If not, you will need to work some more until your work is good.
- Keep all your work in your ticket folder until it is all due on Friday, then turn in your folder when the teacher asks for it.
- You will need to meet with the teacher when she calls your name during the week. That's the Teacher Feature. The teacher will help you and some of your classmates with your math during the Teacher Feature and will see how you are doing with your ticket.
- Your ticket grade will come from four places:

    1. How hard you work during ticket time every day,
    2. Whether you finish your ticket work on time,
    3. One piece of work you select to represent your understanding,
    4. One piece of work the teacher picks randomly from your ticket folder.

Work hard and help your friends do the same. This is a chance for you to show how good you are in managing your time, making plans, and doing math!

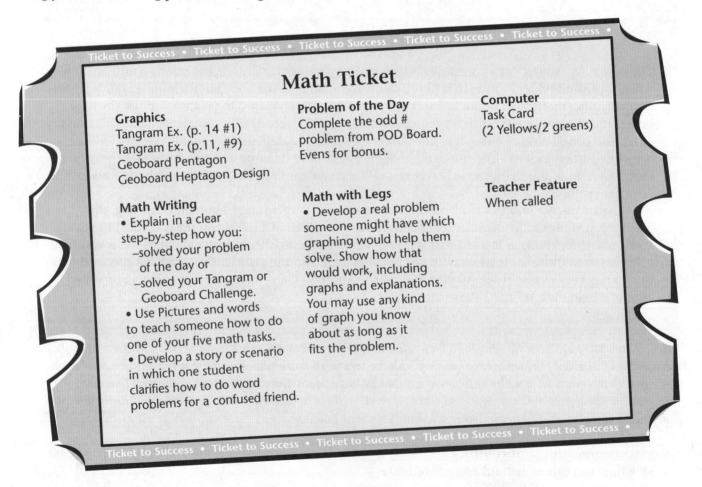

Math Ticket

Graphics
Tangram Ex. (p. 14 #1)
Tangram Ex. (p.11, #9)
Geoboard Pentagon
Geoboard Heptagon Design

Math Writing
- Explain in a clear step-by-step how you:
    - solved your problem of the day or
    - solved your Tangram or Geoboard Challenge.
- Use Pictures and words to teach someone how to do one of your five math tasks.
- Develop a story or scenario in which one student clarifies how to do word problems for a confused friend.

Problem of the Day
Complete the odd # problem from POD Board. Evens for bonus.

Math with Legs
- Develop a real problem someone might have which graphing would help them solve. Show how that would work, including graphs and explanations. You may use any kind of graph you know about as long as it fits the problem.

Computer
Task Card
(2 Yellows/2 greens)

Teacher Feature
When called

Source: Adapted by permission of Pearly de Leon, Chapel Hill-Carroboro City Schools, Chapel Hill, NC

FIGURE T.23

ThinkDots

Explanation: After students have worked to gain essential knowledge, understanding, and skill about a topic, they can use a versatile strategy called ThinkDots to review, demonstrate, and extend their thinking on the subject. Developed by Kay Brimijoin in 1999, ThinkDots is a modification of the strategy called cubing (Neeld, 1988). The modifications make the approach teacher-friendly, while at the same time allowing for maximum flexibility in terms of differentiation. Unlike paper cubes that are often fragile, even when laminated, or plastic picture cubes that can be costly for large classes, ThinkDots are inexpensive, easy to construct, and compact for storage.

A ThinkDots set consists of six cards that are hole punched in one corner. The set is held together with a "notebook ring," a loop of string, or any other device that allows students to flip through the set easily. Each card has one or more dots on its front (each card corresponding to one of the six dot configurations on a die). On the back of each card is a question or task that asks students to work directly with important knowledge, understanding, and skill related to the topic they are studying. Dots are easily drawn on cards, or can be quickly created using small paper disks. Laminating the cards enables teacher and students to use them more than once during a year or unit, and allows teachers to use them in successive years.

ThinkDots can be used to respond to learner readiness by developing ThinkDots tasks at varying levels of difficulty. In addition, ThinkDots can be used to respond to learning profiles by developing prompts based on varied intelligence preferences, requiring different modes of expression, or even by encouraging students to work alone or collaboratively with ThinkDots tasks. ThinkDots questions can also invite learners to apply key ideas and skills based on interest or choice.

For example, in one setting, teachers might place students of somewhat similar readiness levels together with a ThinkDots set designed to review and extend key goals at a level of difficulty challenging for that group. In another setting, the teacher might design ThinkDots sets to correspond to students' learning preferences, with one group expressing ideas through visual modes, another through more kinesthetic modes, another in writing, and so on.

To address interests, students might select a group, for example, representing a particular interest in music, sports, science, and so forth. ThinkDots tasks in this instance would ask students to see how ideas studied in the unit apply to their particular interest. For example, in a unit on fractions, ThinkDots questions could ask students to find out how fractions are used in a sport, develop a brief scenario showing how fractions work in action in the sport, explain how the sport would change if fractions ceased to exist, and so on.

To address learning profile, students might select a group based on a preferred mode of learning (visual, practical, kinesthetic, reading, and others) and work with peers with the same preference. Students in all groups would address the same essential learning goals, but ThinkDots tasks would aid them in exploring and expressing ideas in ways that are most effective for them.

The procedure for implementing ThinkDots includes the following:

- The teacher determines the key knowledge, understanding, or skill with which the ThinkDots strategy will be used.
- The teacher reviews students' readiness levels, interests, and learning profiles and assigns students to groups based on needs and learning goals.
- Each student or group receives a set of activities, a die, and an activity log.
- Students roll the die and complete activities marked with dots that correspond to the dots rolled on the die. Students may be asked to roll their die one to six times and complete the corresponding tasks.

Generally, a student can complete only one or two tasks when the tasks are more complex, but it is feasible to expect each to complete multiple tasks when the tasks are less complex and multi-faceted or when students complete review and extension questions. In some cases, it might be appropriate for all students to complete a designated "core" ThinkDots task targeting key learning goals for the unit or lesson, then to complete other tasks as indicated by rolling the die.

* Each student then records answers or results in their activity log and attaches any additional material required to show work process, steps in thinking, resources consulted, and so on.

Because students will not complete all tasks in the set, it is important that each task require them to work with the unit's essential knowledge, understanding, and skill. It is also very helpful to have students share their work with peers to have the key goals reinforced by seeing them explored through various approaches. Careful and systematic collaboration is imperative if varied tasks call on only selected essential unit goals so that students explore ideas they "missed" in their own work by learning from peers. In these instances, it is particularly necessary for teachers to bring common closure to the ThinkDots process so that all students are comfortable with all key outcomes. Such closure not only helps students understand they are working toward common goals, but also gives them an opportunity to take part in a teacher-guided review of all the lesson's key ideas and skills, even though the student may not have worked directly with all of those ideas and skills in the ThinkDots activity.

ThinkDots EXAMPLE 1

The ThinkDots example that follows was developed by a 6th grade teacher whose students were studying matter in science. The activity was used as a review to give students an opportunity to apply and extend their understanding of the unit's key goals. The unit and activity are carefully keyed to state standards. Below are standards related to the activity, learning goals based on the standards, and the two versions of the ThinkDots activity. The second set is more complex than the first, but both require students to think about, apply, and extend the same essential knowledge, understanding, and skill. The teacher assigned students to one of the tasks based on assessment throughout the unit. The teacher met with all students who worked on the first ThinkDots assignments and then with students who worked on the second ThinkDots assignments to ensure clarity of understanding after the small groups shared their work. It would also have worked well to conduct a closure discussion with the class as a whole.

Science Standards of Learning (Virginia)
- 6.5 Matter is made up of atoms.
- 6.5 Atoms are made up of electrons, protons, and neutrons.
- 6.6 Materials can be classified as elements, compounds, or mixtures.
- 6.7a and 6.7b Matter can undergo physical and chemical changes.

As a result of the activity, students will

Know
- The structure of atoms, their parts, and functions.
- The characteristics of specific elements and compounds.
- The properties of physical and chemical changes.
- The Periodic Table (definition, explanation).

Understand
- The structure of an atom can determine whether it is a specific element or compound.
- Elements can combine physically or chemically to create new structures.
- The Periodic Table is a scientific tool that helps us study how the structures of elements are alike and different.

Be able to
- Discuss the characteristics of atoms.
- Show how the properties of an element are related to its position in the Periodic Table.
- Analyze physical and chemical properties and changes.
- Discuss and work collaboratively.

Directions: *Work with your group of three to check your knowledge of matter and to apply what you have learned. Take turns rolling a die until all six tasks are taken. Each of you will have two tasks to complete. Ask one another for help if you get stuck. On Wednesday, you will need to be ready to share your work with the others in your group. Use your activity log to make notes on what you will tell your group about each task. Write questions in the log also that will help you and them see if they really understand what you have shared with them. The questions should be understanding questions, not just fact questions.*

ThinkDots Version 1: Matter

What is the correct symbol for the element helium? Research the history of this element and create a time-line showing what elements were discovered just before and after helium.	Name three types of physical changes. Create a list with at least two examples of each that are different from the examples in the book.	Which is higher, an element's atomic number or its mass number? Why?
Share two ways that scientists study atoms. Suggest and explain new ways you can think of to study atoms.	How are physical and chemical properties different? Why?	What does the periodic table tell us about calcium? How can this help us in our everyday lives?

ThinkDots Version 2: Matter

How do the atomic numbers in the periodic table change from the top to the bottom? From left to right across the table?	Predict as many properties for potassium as you can. To make your predictions, look at the information in the box for this element and consider its location on the periodic table.	Carbon is atomic number 6. How are two carbon atoms with mass numbers of 12 and 14 different? Why are these atoms called isotopes?
Why do you think scientists used the term "cloud" to describe the position of electrons in an atom?	Suppose you were given some sugar cubes, a grinder, some water, a pan, and a hot plate. What physical and chemical changes could you make in the sugar?	There are three jars in the front of the room. Each has a substance with a strong odor. One is a solid, one is a liquid, and one is a gas. Which odor would students in the back of the room smell first? Why?

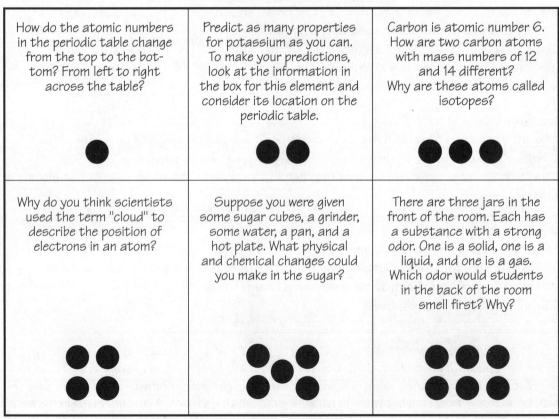

Source: Based on example developed by and used with permission of Pat Goolsby, Amherst County (Virginia) Schools.

ThinkDots EXAMPLE 2

This example of ThinkDots was developed by an algebra teacher who used the strategy as a format for generating group discussion on particular learning goals. Students worked in groups of approximately four. Each group had a "roller" and a "scribe." The roller not only rolled the die and read the ThinkDots problem that matched the die, but also facilitated the discussion of the group on the problem. Once the problem was read, students worked as a group to solve the problem. The scribe wrote the ideas of the group and recorded the steps and solution they developed for the problem. The roller then got the teacher's answer key and the group checked their work, discussing its thoroughness and accuracy.

In the examples below, groups worked their way through all five problems in the order they rolled the corresponding numbers. At other times, students might be asked to discuss and solve three problems, for example, in a specified time. This same process could be used for a group assessment, with the group rolling and solving one problem in a specified length of time. Here, the teacher gave different ThinkDots sets to different groups based on task readiness. In other instances, the teacher may prefer to use somewhat more heterogeneous groups for review, with groups including students who are better at solving computations, better at word problems, and better at mathematical writing.

The teacher can collect the "scribe sheets" to gain insight into the students' thinking processes.

ThinkDots Version 1: Solving Equations

a, b, and c each represent a different value. If a=2, find b, c, and d. $a + b = c$ $a - c = d$ $a + b = 5$	Explain the mathematical reasoning involved in solving the problem on Card 1.	Create an interesting word problem modeled by $8x - 2 = 7$.
Explain in words what the equation $2x + 4 = 10$ means. Solve the problem.	Create an interesting word problem that is modeled by $8x - 2 = 7x$.	Explain what changing the "3" in $3x = 9$ does to the value of x. Why is this true?

ThinkDots Version 2: Solving Equations

a, b, and c each represent a different value. If a = -1, find b, c, and d. $a + b = c$ $b + b = d$ $c - a = {}^-a$ ●	Explain the mathematical reasoning involved in solving the problem on Card 1. ● ●	Explain how a variable is used to solve word problems. ● ● ●
Diagram how to solve $3x + 1 = 10$. ● ● ● ●	Create an interesting word problem that is modeled by $2x + 4 = 4x - 10$. Solve the problem. ● ● ● ●	Explain why x = 4 in 2x = 8 but x = 16 in 1/2 x = 8. Why does this make sense? ● ● ● ● ● ●

ThinkDots Version 3: Solving Equations

a, b, and c each represent a different value. If a=4, find b, c, and d. $a + c = b$ $b - a = c$ $cd = {}^-d$ $d + d = a$ ●	Explain the mathematical reasoning involved in solving the problem on Card 1. ● ●	Create an interesting word problem modeled by $3x - 1 < 5x + 7$. Solve the problem. ● ● ●
Explain the role of a variable in mathematics. Give examples. ● ● ● ●	Diagram how to solve $3x + 4 = x + 12$. ● ● ● ●	Given ax = 15, explain how x is changed if a is large or a is small in value. ● ● ● ● ● ●

Source: Developed by and used with permission of Nanci Smith, Scottsdale, AZ.

FIGURE T.24

Multiple-Entry Journals

Explanation: A multiple-entry journal provides a structure to guide students' reading by promoting focus, concentration, and thought as they read. When multiple-entry journals are carefully designed, they can be powerful tools to help students become more proficient in using text material effectively.

Two examples of multiple-entry journals follow. The first example could be modified for use from elementary through high school in any subject that calls on students to read and make meaning of print material. The second is a high school math example designed to help students think more flexibly and fully about particular computational approaches and their applications. Both examples are tiered. In each instance, the second tier is more demanding and designed for more advanced students. The first tier calls on students to work with grade-level expectations. Additional tiers could be created as necessary. Note that designations like "basic" or "advanced" would not appear on student copies.

JOURNAL EXAMPLE 1

This format calls on students to look for certain elements in a chapter as they read and then to reflect on certain elements after they read. At any point when students use the multiple-entry journals, the teacher indicates elements on which they should focus both as and after reading.

The more basic version provided first is geared to the reading needs of students who struggle to some degree with text materials. Because this version is very flexible, teachers can spotlight different skills for different learners—and change prompts with particular assignments as student needs become evident. Teachers may select from prompts such as the following for this version, which is just one sample of how a multiple-entry journal might be structured.

Sample "As You Read" Prompts for Basic Version	Sample "After You Read" Prompts for Basic Version
Key phrases	How to use ideas or information
Important words	Why particular words are important
Main ideas	A prediction based on current information
Puzzling passages	Why a passage seems puzzling
Summaries of sections	A reaction to a passage
Passages that seem powerful	Personal experience that connects with a passage
Key parts of the chapter	A comment on the author's view or style
Interpretation of graphics	How graphics connect with the text
Beginning, middle (with detail), end	Meanings of key words
Connections with what you already know	What a puzzling passage seems to mean
Questions you have as you read	
Things you find interesting	

For the more advanced version, students have a three-column format. The prompts ensure focus on basic elements of the text, but push students ahead to grapple with more abstract elements stated and unstated in the text. For the more advanced version, the teacher might select from prompts such as the following.

As You Read	As You Read or After You Read	After You Read
Key passages Key vocabulary Organizing concepts Key principles Key patterns	Why particular ideas are important How the author has developed his line of logic, thought, or argument How parts and whole relate Assumptions of the author, especially those that probe for deeper understanding Connections with other subjects and areas of life	Hypothesize what a person might actually say to you about what's in the reading; for example: • The teacher • The author • An expert in the field • A character • A satirist • A political cartoonist • Someone with a different perspective on the topic

Version 1 (Basic Version)
Multiple-Entry Journal

Directions: *As you read today, look for the items in the left column and make notes on what you find. Then after you read, reflect on the items in the right column and record your thoughts.*

As You Read	*After You Read*
Important words Main ideas Key parts of the chapter	Predictions about what we'll emphasize in class based on your reading Why you selected the ideas you did as being main ideas

Version 2 (Advanced Version)
Multiple-Entry Journal

Directions: *As you read today, look for the items in the left column and make notes on what you find. Look for items in the center column as you read or after you read and make notes on them in the center column. Then after you read, reflect on the prompt in the right column and record your thoughts.*

As You Read	As You Read or After You Read	After You Read
Key passages Organizing concepts	Why certain ideas are important How parts and whole relate	What you think the following would say about the contents of the assigned reading: • An expert in the field • A satirist

JOURNAL EXAMPLE 2

This example asks high school math students to think about and apply what they have been learning in trigonometry. The format encourages students to do math reasoning and writing.

The more basic version provides a problem, designates two ways in which students should solve the problem, and asks for an application of principles to a more authentic context. The more advanced version leaves the two solutions to the problem up to students, asks which solution is the more efficient and which is the more elegant, and asks students to develop a real world application themselves.

Note again that designations like "basic" or "advanced" would not appear on student copies.

Version 1 (Basic Version)
Multiple-Entry Journal

Directions: *This journal page is designed to help you draw on and apply what you have been learning in trigonometry. Column 1 provides you with a problem. Columns 2 and 3 ask you to solve the problem in two different ways. Column 4 asks you to apply one of the strategies to solve a similar problem that might occur outside the classroom. Write your work and explanations carefully and fully in columns 2, 3, and 4.*

The Problem	Strategy 1 for Solving the Problem	Strategy 2 for Solving the Problem	Solving and Explaining a Real World Problem
Find the missing side of the triangle. 13' 15' 60.07° X	Solve using trigonometry and explain your thinking.	Solve using the Pythagorean Theorem and explain your thinking.	Will a tree of _____ (dimensions) hit a house of _____(distance) away if it's cut down and falls in the direction of the house?

Version 1 (Advanced Version)
Multiple-Entry Journal

Directions: *This journal page is designed to help you draw on and apply what you have been learning in trigonometry. Column 1 provides you with a problem. Columns 2 and 3 ask you to solve the problem in two different ways. As you select ways you might solve the problem and use those approaches to solve it, also explain which of the two approaches you feel is the more efficient (and why) and which you feel is the more elegant (and why). Column 4 asks you to develop and solve a problem that might occur outside the classroom and that is similar to the visual problem in Column 1. You may solve the problem in column 4 in any appropriate way. Write your work and explanations carefully and fully in columns 2, 3, and 4.*

The Problem	Strategy 1 for Solving the Problem	Strategy 2 for Solving the Problem	Statement, Solution, and Explanation of a Related Real-World Problem
Find the missing side of the triangle. 13' 15' 60.07° X	Select, use, and explain one way to solve the problem.	Select, use, and explain a second way to solve the problem. Explain which of the two solutions is more elegant and which is more efficient and why you say so.	Develop and solve a problem related to the triangle problem in column 1. Explain your solution.

Index

Note: Page numbers followed by *f* are figures.

163

About the Author

Carol Ann Tomlinson is Professor of Educational Leadership, Foundations, and Policy at the University of Virginia and was a public school teacher for 21 years. In 1974, she was chosen Virginia's Teacher of the Year. While working in public school, she taught in many differentiated classrooms and directed district-level programs for struggling and advanced learners. Today, as Co-Director of the University of Virginia Summer Institute on Academic Diversity, she works with an international community of educators committed to academically responsive classrooms.

Tomlinson has authored several books for ASCD, including *How to Differentiate Instruction in Mixed-Ability Classrooms; The Differentiated Classroom;* (with Susan Allan) *Leadership for Differentiating Schools and Classrooms;* and (with Caroline Cunningham-Eidson) *Differentiation in Practice: A Resource Guide for Differentiating Curriculum, Grades 5–9* and *Differentiation in Practice: A Resource Guide for Differentiating Curriculum, Grades K–5.* She consulted on and authored facilitator guides for five ASCD video staff development sets and developed ASCD's Professional Inquiry Kit on Differentiated Instruction.

Tomlinson can be reached at the Curry School of Education, The University of Virginia, P.O. Box 400277, Charlottesville, VA, 22904, or via e-mail at cat3y@virginia.edu.

Related ASCD Resources: Fulfilling the Promise of the Differentiated Classroom: Strategies and Tools for Responsive Teaching

At the time of publication, the following ASCD resources were available; for the most up-to-date information about ASCD resources, go to www.ascd.org. ASCD stock numbers are noted in parentheses.

Audiotapes

All Kids Learn the Same . . . Differently! by Marilee Sprenger (#203192) **Also on CD!**

Annual Conference 2003 Audios Complete Set (23 tapes) (#203306) **Also on CD!**

Coaching for Differentiation by Carol O'Connor (#203161) **Also on CD!**

Connecting Research to Practice: Improving Achievement for Diverse Learners by Vera Blake and Maria Montalvo (#200128)

Coteaching a Differentiated Language Arts Curriculum by Barbara Menzies, Ann Murray Orr, Ruthanne Tobin (#201197)

Creating Universal Access Within the Differentiated Classroom by Shirley Gilfether and Dan Herlihy (#202257)

Designing Staff Development to Encourage Differentiated Instruction by Leslie J. Kiernan and Carol Ann Tomlinson (#201160)

Differentiating Curriculum and Assessment for Mixed-Ability Classrooms by Carol Ann Tomlinson (#298309)

Differentiated Instruction for Oral Reading in Bilingual Classrooms by Luz Stella Lopez (#503290) **Also on CD!**

District, School, and Classroom Supports for Differentiated Instruction by Sandra L. Delaney, David Castelline, and Lisa Mikus (#202246)

Diversity by Design: Differentiation and Integration in Classrooms That Work by Harvey F. Silver (2 tapes) (#503263) **Also on CD!**

Energizing and Sustaining the Move Toward Differentiated Classrooms by Carol Ann Tomlinson (#503294) **Also on CD!**

Providing Leadership for Differentiated Classrooms by Carol Ann Tomlinson (#200084)

Teaching Students with High Academic Ability in Mixed-Ability Classrooms by Susan Winebrenner (#299060)

Understanding by Design and Differentiated Instruction: Partners in Classroom by Grant Wiggins, Jay McTighe and Carol Ann Tomlinson (#503281) **Also on CD!**

Multimedia

ASCD Professional Development Planner: Differentiated Instruction and Resource Package (#701225)

Differentiating Instruction for Mixed-Ability Classrooms Professional Inquiry Kit by Carol Ann Tomlinson (eight activity folders and a videotape) (#196213)

Networks

Visit the ASCD Web site (www.ascd.org) and search for "networks" for information about professional educators who have formed groups around topics like "Differentiated Instruction." Look in the "Network Directory" for current facilitators' addresses and phone numbers.

Online Resources

Visit ASCD's Web site (www.ascd.org) for the following professional development opportunities:

Online Tutorial: *Differentiating Instruction* (free)
Professional Development Online: *Differentiating Instruction,* among others (for a small fee; password protected)

Print Products

Curriculum Update: Differentiating Instruction (entire issue, Winter 2000) (#100024)

The Differentiated Classroom: Responding to the Needs of All Learners by Carol Ann Tomlinson (#199040)

Differentiation in Practice: A Resource Guide for Differentiating Curriculum, Grades K–5 by Carol Ann Tomlinson and Caroline Cunningham Eidson (#102294) **NEW!**

Differentiation in Practice: A Resource Guide for Differentiating Curriculum, Grades 5–9 by Carol Ann Tomlinson and Caroline Cunningham Eidson (#102293)

Differentiated Instruction Topic Pack (print and electronic versions available) Revised for 2001–2002 (#101032)

Educational Leadership: Do Students Care About Learning? (entire issue, September 2002) Excerpted articles online free; entire issue online and accessible to ASCD members

How to Differentiate Instruction in Mixed-Ability Classrooms, 2nd Edition by Carol Ann Tomlinson (#101043)

Leadership for Differentiating Schools and Classrooms by Susan Demirskay Allan and Carol Ann Tomlinson (#100216)

Motivating Students and Teachers in an Era of Standards by Richard Sagor (#103009) **NEW!**

Videos

Differentiating Instruction Video Series with Facilitator's Guide, How to Differentiate Instruction Book Educational consultant: Carol Ann Tomlinson (#497023)

Instructional Strategies for the Differentiated Classroom (4 videos and facilitator's guide) (#403330) **NEW!**

A Visit to a Differentiated Classroom (#401309)

At Work in the Differentiated Classroom Video Series (3 videos with a facilitator's guide) Educational consultant: Carol Ann Tomlinson (#401071) **NEW!**

For more information, visit us on the World Wide Web (http://www.ascd.org), send an e-mail message to member@ascd.org, call the ASCD Service Center (1-800-933-ASCD or 703-578-9600, then press 2), send a fax to 703-575-5400, or write to Information Services, ASCD, 1703 N. Beauregard St., Alexandria, VA 22311-1714 USA.